50 Cake Decorative Recipes for Home

By: Kelly Johnson

Table of Contents

- Rainbow Layer Cake
- Floral Buttercream Cake
- Chocolate Ganache Drip Cake
- Ombre Ruffle Cake
- Geode Cake
- Mirror Glaze Cake
- Fault Line Cake
- Naked Cake with Fresh Fruit
- Galaxy Cake
- Watercolor Buttercream Cake
- Sprinkle Explosion Cake
- Gold Leaf Cake
- Succulent Garden Cake
- Unicorn Cake
- Drip Cake with Macarons
- Buttercream Flower Wreath Cake
- Painted Buttercream Cake
- Pinata Cake
- Marbled Fondant Cake
- Gravity-Defying Cake
- Candy Land Cake
- Chalkboard Cake
- Topsy-Turvy Cake
- Mermaid Tail Cake
- Cookie Monster Cake
- Woodland Creature Cake
- Llama Cake
- Vintage Lace Cake
- Tropical Tiki Cake
- Zebra Striped Cake
- Balloon Cake
- Emoji Cake
- Puzzle Piece Cake
- Stained Glass Cake
- Dinosaur Fossil Cake

- Circus Tent Cake
- Pop Art Cake
- Pirate Ship Cake
- Underwater Sea Creature Cake
- Comic Book Cake
- Edible Flower Petal Cake
- Rainbow Swirl Cake
- Rose Gold Cake
- Floral Crown Cake
- Avocado Cake
- Camping Tent Cake
- Space Rocket Cake
- Dia de los Muertos Cake
- Harry Potter Sorting Hat Cake
- Vintage Travel Suitcase Cake

Rainbow Layer Cake

Ingredients:

For the cake layers:

- 2 cups all-purpose flour
- 2 teaspoons baking powder
- 1/2 teaspoon salt
- 3/4 cup unsalted butter, at room temperature
- 1 1/2 cups granulated sugar
- 4 large eggs, at room temperature
- 1 tablespoon vanilla extract
- 1 cup whole milk

For the rainbow colors:

- Gel food coloring in red, orange, yellow, green, blue, and purple

For the frosting:

- 1 1/2 cups unsalted butter, at room temperature
- 6 cups powdered sugar
- 1/4 cup heavy cream
- 1 tablespoon vanilla extract
- Pinch of salt

Instructions:

1. Preheat your oven to 350°F (175°C). Grease and flour three 8-inch round cake pans and line the bottoms with parchment paper.
2. In a medium bowl, whisk together the flour, baking powder, and salt. Set aside.
3. In a large mixing bowl, cream together the butter and sugar until light and fluffy using a hand mixer or stand mixer.
4. Add the eggs one at a time, mixing well after each addition. Stir in the vanilla extract.

5. Gradually add the dry ingredients to the wet ingredients, alternating with the milk, beginning and ending with the dry ingredients. Mix until just combined.
6. Divide the batter evenly into six bowls. Add a few drops of gel food coloring to each bowl to create red, orange, yellow, green, blue, and purple batters. Stir until the colors are evenly distributed.
7. Pour each colored batter into a separate cake pan and spread evenly.
8. Bake in the preheated oven for 18-22 minutes, or until a toothpick inserted into the center of the cakes comes out clean.
9. Allow the cakes to cool in the pans for 10 minutes, then transfer them to a wire rack to cool completely.
10. While the cakes are cooling, prepare the frosting. In a large mixing bowl, beat the butter until creamy. Gradually add the powdered sugar, alternating with the heavy cream, vanilla extract, and salt. Beat until smooth and creamy.
11. Once the cakes are completely cooled, assemble the rainbow layer cake by stacking the layers with a thin layer of frosting between each one.
12. Frost the top and sides of the cake with the remaining frosting, smoothing it out with a spatula.
13. Slice and serve the rainbow layer cake, and enjoy the colorful and delicious dessert!

Feel free to adjust the colors and decorations to suit your preferences and occasion.

Floral Buttercream Cake

Ingredients:

For the cake:

- 2 cups all-purpose flour
- 2 teaspoons baking powder
- 1/2 teaspoon salt
- 3/4 cup unsalted butter, at room temperature
- 1 1/2 cups granulated sugar
- 4 large eggs, at room temperature
- 1 tablespoon vanilla extract
- 1 cup whole milk

For the buttercream frosting:

- 2 cups unsalted butter, at room temperature
- 4 cups powdered sugar
- 2 teaspoons vanilla extract
- Pinch of salt
- Gel food coloring (optional)
- Assorted edible flowers for decoration

Instructions:

1. Preheat your oven to 350°F (175°C). Grease and flour three 8-inch round cake pans and line the bottoms with parchment paper.
2. In a medium bowl, whisk together the flour, baking powder, and salt. Set aside.
3. In a large mixing bowl, cream together the butter and sugar until light and fluffy using a hand mixer or stand mixer.
4. Add the eggs one at a time, mixing well after each addition. Stir in the vanilla extract.
5. Gradually add the dry ingredients to the wet ingredients, alternating with the milk, beginning and ending with the dry ingredients. Mix until just combined.
6. Divide the batter evenly into the prepared cake pans and spread it out evenly.

7. Bake in the preheated oven for 18-22 minutes, or until a toothpick inserted into the center of the cakes comes out clean.
8. Allow the cakes to cool in the pans for 10 minutes, then transfer them to a wire rack to cool completely.
9. While the cakes are cooling, prepare the buttercream frosting. In a large mixing bowl, beat the butter until creamy. Gradually add the powdered sugar, vanilla extract, and salt. Beat until smooth and creamy. Add gel food coloring if desired for a tinted frosting.
10. Once the cakes are completely cooled, assemble the cake by stacking the layers with a thin layer of frosting between each one.
11. Apply a thin layer of frosting around the entire cake to create a crumb coat. This will seal in any crumbs.
12. Chill the cake in the refrigerator for about 30 minutes to set the crumb coat.
13. Once the crumb coat is set, apply a final layer of frosting around the cake, smoothing it out with a spatula.
14. Using a piping bag fitted with a flower tip, pipe buttercream flowers around the top and sides of the cake. You can use different colors to create a vibrant floral design.
15. Decorate the cake with assorted edible flowers, placing them among the piped buttercream flowers for a beautiful finishing touch.
16. Slice and serve the floral buttercream cake, and enjoy the delicious and elegant dessert!

This cake is perfect for weddings, bridal showers, or any special occasion where you want to impress with both taste and presentation.

Chocolate Ganache Drip Cake

Ingredients:

For the chocolate cake:

- 2 cups all-purpose flour
- 1 3/4 cups granulated sugar
- 3/4 cup unsweetened cocoa powder
- 2 teaspoons baking powder
- 1 teaspoon baking soda
- 1 teaspoon salt
- 2 large eggs, at room temperature
- 1 cup whole milk
- 1/2 cup vegetable oil
- 2 teaspoons vanilla extract
- 1 cup boiling water

For the chocolate ganache:

- 1 cup heavy cream
- 8 ounces semi-sweet chocolate, finely chopped

Instructions:

1. Preheat your oven to 350°F (175°C). Grease and flour three 8-inch round cake pans and line the bottoms with parchment paper.
2. In a large mixing bowl, sift together the flour, sugar, cocoa powder, baking powder, baking soda, and salt.
3. Add the eggs, milk, oil, and vanilla extract to the dry ingredients and mix until smooth.
4. Stir in the boiling water until the batter is well combined. The batter will be thin.
5. Divide the batter evenly among the prepared cake pans.
6. Bake in the preheated oven for 25-30 minutes, or until a toothpick inserted into the center of the cakes comes out clean.
7. Allow the cakes to cool in the pans for 10 minutes, then transfer them to a wire rack to cool completely.
8. While the cakes are cooling, prepare the chocolate ganache. In a small saucepan, heat the heavy cream over medium heat until it begins to simmer.

9. Place the chopped chocolate in a heatproof bowl. Pour the hot cream over the chocolate and let it sit for 2-3 minutes.
10. Stir the chocolate and cream together until smooth and glossy. Let the ganache cool slightly to thicken.
11. Once the cakes are completely cooled, level the tops if necessary to create flat surfaces.
12. Place one cake layer on a serving plate or cake stand. Spread a layer of ganache on top of the cake.
13. Place another cake layer on top and repeat the process until all layers are stacked, reserving some ganache for the drip.
14. Use the remaining ganache to create a drip effect around the edges of the cake. Let the ganache drip down the sides naturally.
15. Once the ganache has set slightly, decorate the top of the cake with any additional decorations or toppings you desire, such as chocolate curls or sprinkles.
16. Slice and serve the chocolate ganache drip cake, and enjoy the rich and indulgent dessert!

This cake is sure to impress with its glossy ganache drip and intense chocolate flavor.

Ombre Ruffle Cake

Ingredients:

For the cake layers:

- 2 cups all-purpose flour
- 1 1/2 cups granulated sugar
- 1 tablespoon baking powder
- 1/2 teaspoon salt
- 3/4 cup unsalted butter, softened
- 1 cup whole milk
- 4 large eggs
- 1 tablespoon vanilla extract

For the buttercream frosting:

- 3 cups unsalted butter, softened
- 6 cups powdered sugar
- 2 teaspoons vanilla extract
- Pinch of salt
- Gel food coloring in your desired ombre shades

Instructions:

1. Preheat your oven to 350°F (175°C). Grease and flour three 8-inch round cake pans and line the bottoms with parchment paper.
2. In a large mixing bowl, cream together the butter and sugar until light and fluffy using a hand mixer or stand mixer.
3. Add the eggs one at a time, mixing well after each addition. Stir in the vanilla extract.
4. In a separate bowl, sift together the flour, baking powder, and salt.
5. Gradually add the dry ingredients to the wet ingredients, alternating with the milk, beginning and ending with the dry ingredients. Mix until just combined.
6. Divide the batter evenly into three bowls. Add gel food coloring to each bowl to create your desired ombre shades, starting with the lightest shade and gradually adding more color to each bowl.

7. Pour each colored batter into the prepared cake pans and spread evenly.
8. Bake in the preheated oven for 18-22 minutes, or until a toothpick inserted into the center of the cakes comes out clean.
9. Allow the cakes to cool in the pans for 10 minutes, then transfer them to a wire rack to cool completely.
10. While the cakes are cooling, prepare the buttercream frosting. In a large mixing bowl, beat the butter until creamy. Gradually add the powdered sugar, vanilla extract, and salt. Beat until smooth and creamy.
11. Once the cakes are completely cooled, level the tops if necessary to create flat surfaces.
12. Place one cake layer on a serving plate or cake stand. Spread a thin layer of frosting on top.
13. Repeat with the remaining layers, stacking them on top of each other.
14. Apply a thin layer of frosting around the entire cake to create a crumb coat. This will seal in any crumbs.
15. Chill the cake in the refrigerator for about 30 minutes to set the crumb coat.
16. Once the crumb coat is set, apply a final layer of frosting around the cake, smoothing it out with a spatula.
17. To create the ombre ruffle effect, fill a piping bag fitted with a petal tip with the darkest shade of frosting. Starting from the bottom of the cake, pipe overlapping ruffles around the entire circumference of the cake, gradually switching to lighter shades as you work your way up.
18. Continue piping ruffles until the entire cake is covered in a beautiful ombre effect.
19. Slice and serve the ombre ruffle cake, and enjoy the stunning and delicious dessert!

This cake is sure to be a showstopper at any special occasion with its gorgeous gradient colors and intricate texture.

Geode Cake

Ingredients:

For the cake layers:

- 3 cups all-purpose flour
- 3 cups granulated sugar
- 1 cup unsweetened cocoa powder
- 1 tablespoon baking soda
- 1 1/2 teaspoons baking powder
- 1 1/2 teaspoons salt
- 4 large eggs, at room temperature
- 1 1/2 cups buttermilk, at room temperature
- 1 1/2 cups warm water
- 1/2 cup vegetable oil
- 2 teaspoons vanilla extract

For the frosting:

- 3 cups unsalted butter, softened
- 6 cups powdered sugar
- 1/2 cup heavy cream
- 2 teaspoons vanilla extract
- Pinch of salt
- Gel food coloring in your desired geode colors (typically blue, purple, and white)

For the geode:

- 1 cup granulated sugar
- 1/2 cup water
- Gel food coloring in your desired geode colors
- Edible gold or silver leaf (optional)

Instructions:

1. Preheat your oven to 350°F (175°C). Grease and flour three 8-inch round cake pans and line the bottoms with parchment paper.
2. In a large mixing bowl, sift together the flour, sugar, cocoa powder, baking soda, baking powder, and salt.
3. In a separate bowl, whisk together the eggs, buttermilk, warm water, oil, and vanilla extract.
4. Gradually add the wet ingredients to the dry ingredients, mixing until smooth and well combined.
5. Divide the batter evenly among the prepared cake pans.
6. Bake in the preheated oven for 30-35 minutes, or until a toothpick inserted into the center of the cakes comes out clean.
7. Allow the cakes to cool in the pans for 10 minutes, then transfer them to a wire rack to cool completely.
8. While the cakes are cooling, prepare the frosting. In a large mixing bowl, beat the butter until creamy. Gradually add the powdered sugar, heavy cream, vanilla extract, and salt. Beat until smooth and creamy.
9. Once the cakes are completely cooled, level the tops if necessary to create flat surfaces.
10. Place one cake layer on a serving plate or cake stand. Spread a layer of frosting on top.
11. Repeat with the remaining layers, stacking them on top of each other.
12. Apply a thin layer of frosting around the entire cake to create a crumb coat. This will seal in any crumbs.
13. Chill the cake in the refrigerator for about 30 minutes to set the crumb coat.
14. Once the crumb coat is set, apply a final layer of frosting around the cake, smoothing it out with a spatula.
15. To create the geode, combine the granulated sugar and water in a small saucepan over medium heat. Stir until the sugar is dissolved.
16. Bring the mixture to a boil, then reduce the heat to low and simmer until it reaches 300°F (150°C) on a candy thermometer, about 10-15 minutes.
17. Remove the mixture from the heat and stir in gel food coloring to achieve your desired geode colors.
18. Carefully pour the colored sugar mixture onto a parchment-lined baking sheet, creating irregular shapes to resemble geodes.
19. Let the sugar geodes cool and harden completely.
20. Once the geodes are cooled and hardened, gently press them into the sides of the cake to create the geode effect.
21. If desired, add edible gold or silver leaf to enhance the geode effect.
22. Slice and serve the geode cake, and enjoy the breathtaking and delicious dessert!

This cake will definitely make a statement at any special occasion with its mesmerizing geode design and rich chocolate flavor.

Mirror Glaze Cake

Ingredients:

For the cake:

- 2 cups all-purpose flour
- 2 cups granulated sugar
- 3/4 cup unsweetened cocoa powder
- 2 teaspoons baking powder
- 1 1/2 teaspoons baking soda
- 1 teaspoon salt
- 2 large eggs, at room temperature
- 1 cup whole milk
- 1/2 cup vegetable oil
- 2 teaspoons vanilla extract
- 1 cup hot water

For the mirror glaze:

- 1/2 cup water
- 1 cup granulated sugar
- 2/3 cup sweetened condensed milk
- 1 1/2 cups white chocolate chips
- 2 tablespoons unflavored gelatin powder
- 1/2 cup cold water
- Gel food coloring (optional)

Instructions:

1. Preheat your oven to 350°F (175°C). Grease and flour three 8-inch round cake pans and line the bottoms with parchment paper.
2. In a large mixing bowl, sift together the flour, sugar, cocoa powder, baking powder, baking soda, and salt.
3. Add the eggs, milk, oil, and vanilla extract to the dry ingredients and mix until smooth.

4. Gradually stir in the hot water until the batter is well combined. The batter will be thin.
5. Divide the batter evenly among the prepared cake pans.
6. Bake in the preheated oven for 25-30 minutes, or until a toothpick inserted into the center of the cakes comes out clean.
7. Allow the cakes to cool in the pans for 10 minutes, then transfer them to a wire rack to cool completely.
8. While the cakes are cooling, prepare the mirror glaze. In a small saucepan, combine 1/2 cup water and 1 cup sugar. Heat over medium heat, stirring constantly, until the sugar is dissolved.
9. Add the sweetened condensed milk and white chocolate chips to the saucepan. Stir until the chocolate is melted and the mixture is smooth. Remove from heat and set aside.
10. In a small bowl, sprinkle the gelatin powder over 1/2 cup cold water. Let it sit for a few minutes to bloom.
11. Once bloomed, heat the gelatin mixture in the microwave for about 30 seconds, or until completely dissolved.
12. Stir the dissolved gelatin into the white chocolate mixture until well combined.
13. If desired, add gel food coloring to the glaze to achieve your desired color.
14. Place a large baking sheet or tray under a wire rack to catch any drips. Place the cooled cakes on the wire rack.
15. Pour the mirror glaze over the cakes, starting from the center and working your way outward in a circular motion, ensuring that the entire cake is covered.
16. Allow the glaze to set for about 30 minutes before transferring the cakes to a serving platter.
17. Slice and serve the mirror glaze cake, and enjoy the stunning and delicious dessert!

The mirror glaze cake will impress with its glossy finish and rich chocolate flavor. Feel free to customize the colors and decorations to suit your preferences and occasion.

Fault Line Cake

Ingredients:

For the cake layers:

- 2 cups all-purpose flour
- 1 3/4 cups granulated sugar
- 3/4 cup unsweetened cocoa powder
- 2 teaspoons baking powder
- 1 1/2 teaspoons baking soda
- 1 teaspoon salt
- 2 large eggs, at room temperature
- 1 cup whole milk
- 1/2 cup vegetable oil
- 2 teaspoons vanilla extract
- 1 cup hot water

For the frosting:

- 3 cups unsalted butter, softened
- 6 cups powdered sugar
- 2 teaspoons vanilla extract
- Pinch of salt
- Gel food coloring in your desired colors for the fault line effect

For the fault line:

- Additional frosting
- Sprinkles, edible pearls, chocolate shards, or other decorations of your choice

Instructions:

1. Preheat your oven to 350°F (175°C). Grease and flour three 8-inch round cake pans and line the bottoms with parchment paper.
2. In a large mixing bowl, sift together the flour, sugar, cocoa powder, baking powder, baking soda, and salt.
3. In a separate bowl, whisk together the eggs, milk, vegetable oil, and vanilla extract.

4. Gradually add the wet ingredients to the dry ingredients, mixing until smooth and well combined.
5. Stir in the hot water until the batter is well combined. The batter will be thin.
6. Divide the batter evenly among the prepared cake pans.
7. Bake in the preheated oven for 30-35 minutes, or until a toothpick inserted into the center of the cakes comes out clean.
8. Allow the cakes to cool in the pans for 10 minutes, then transfer them to a wire rack to cool completely.
9. While the cakes are cooling, prepare the frosting. In a large mixing bowl, beat the butter until creamy. Gradually add the powdered sugar, vanilla extract, and salt. Beat until smooth and creamy.
10. Once the cakes are completely cooled, level the tops if necessary to create flat surfaces.
11. Place one cake layer on a serving plate or cake stand. Spread a layer of frosting on top.
12. Repeat with the remaining layers, stacking them on top of each other.
13. Apply a thin layer of frosting around the entire cake to create a crumb coat. This will seal in any crumbs.
14. Chill the cake in the refrigerator for about 30 minutes to set the crumb coat.
15. Once the crumb coat is set, apply a final layer of frosting around the cake, smoothing it out with a spatula.
16. To create the fault line effect, use a piping bag fitted with a large round tip to pipe a thick line of frosting around the middle of the cake.
17. Use an offset spatula to spread the frosting out slightly, creating a gap in the middle of the cake.
18. Fill the gap with sprinkles, edible pearls, chocolate shards, or other decorations of your choice.
19. If desired, use gel food coloring to add additional color to the fault line frosting.
20. Slice and serve the fault line cake, and enjoy the unique and eye-catching dessert!

The fault line cake is sure to impress with its dramatic design and delicious flavor. Feel free to customize the colors and decorations to suit your preferences and occasion.

Naked Cake with Fresh Fruit

Ingredients:

For the cake layers:

- 2 cups all-purpose flour
- 1 3/4 cups granulated sugar
- 1 tablespoon baking powder
- 1/2 teaspoon salt
- 3/4 cup unsalted butter, softened
- 1 cup whole milk
- 4 large eggs, at room temperature
- 1 tablespoon vanilla extract

For the frosting:

- 2 cups heavy cream
- 1/4 cup powdered sugar
- 1 teaspoon vanilla extract

For the filling and decoration:

- Assorted fresh fruit such as berries, sliced peaches, kiwi, and grapes
- Fresh mint leaves (optional)
- Edible flowers (optional)

Instructions:

1. Preheat your oven to 350°F (175°C). Grease and flour three 8-inch round cake pans and line the bottoms with parchment paper.
2. In a large mixing bowl, sift together the flour, sugar, baking powder, and salt.
3. Add the softened butter to the dry ingredients and mix until the mixture resembles coarse crumbs.
4. In a separate bowl, whisk together the milk, eggs, and vanilla extract.
5. Gradually add the wet ingredients to the dry ingredients, mixing until smooth and well combined.

6. Divide the batter evenly among the prepared cake pans.
7. Bake in the preheated oven for 25-30 minutes, or until a toothpick inserted into the center of the cakes comes out clean.
8. Allow the cakes to cool in the pans for 10 minutes, then transfer them to a wire rack to cool completely.
9. While the cakes are cooling, prepare the frosting. In a large mixing bowl, beat the heavy cream until soft peaks form.
10. Add the powdered sugar and vanilla extract, and continue to beat until stiff peaks form. Be careful not to overbeat.
11. Once the cakes are completely cooled, level the tops if necessary to create flat surfaces.
12. Place one cake layer on a serving plate or cake stand. Spread a layer of whipped cream frosting on top.
13. Repeat with the remaining layers, stacking them on top of each other.
14. Use a spatula to spread a thin layer of frosting around the sides of the cake, leaving the edges exposed to create the naked effect.
15. Decorate the top of the cake with fresh fruit, arranging it in a visually appealing pattern. You can also add fresh mint leaves and edible flowers for additional decoration.
16. Slice and serve the naked cake with fresh fruit, and enjoy the rustic and delicious dessert!

This naked cake with fresh fruit is perfect for summer gatherings, weddings, or any special occasion where you want to impress with both taste and presentation. Feel free to customize the fruit selection and decoration to suit your preferences and occasion.

Galaxy Cake

Ingredients:

For the cake layers:

- 2 cups all-purpose flour
- 1 3/4 cups granulated sugar
- 3/4 cup unsweetened cocoa powder
- 2 teaspoons baking powder
- 1 1/2 teaspoons baking soda
- 1 teaspoon salt
- 2 large eggs, at room temperature
- 1 cup whole milk
- 1/2 cup vegetable oil
- 2 teaspoons vanilla extract
- 1 cup hot water

For the frosting:

- 3 cups unsalted butter, softened
- 6 cups powdered sugar
- 2 teaspoons vanilla extract
- Pinch of salt
- Gel food coloring in dark blue, purple, pink, and black

For the galaxy effect:

- Edible silver or gold stars
- Edible silver or gold dust
- Edible glitter (optional)

Instructions:

1. Preheat your oven to 350°F (175°C). Grease and flour three 8-inch round cake pans and line the bottoms with parchment paper.

2. In a large mixing bowl, sift together the flour, sugar, cocoa powder, baking powder, baking soda, and salt.
3. In a separate bowl, whisk together the eggs, milk, vegetable oil, and vanilla extract.
4. Gradually add the wet ingredients to the dry ingredients, mixing until smooth and well combined.
5. Stir in the hot water until the batter is well combined. The batter will be thin.
6. Divide the batter evenly among the prepared cake pans.
7. Bake in the preheated oven for 30-35 minutes, or until a toothpick inserted into the center of the cakes comes out clean.
8. Allow the cakes to cool in the pans for 10 minutes, then transfer them to a wire rack to cool completely.
9. While the cakes are cooling, prepare the frosting. In a large mixing bowl, beat the butter until creamy. Gradually add the powdered sugar, vanilla extract, and salt. Beat until smooth and creamy.
10. Once the cakes are completely cooled, level the tops if necessary to create flat surfaces.
11. Place one cake layer on a serving plate or cake stand. Spread a layer of frosting on top.
12. Repeat with the remaining layers, stacking them on top of each other.
13. Apply a thin layer of frosting around the entire cake to create a crumb coat. This will seal in any crumbs.
14. Chill the cake in the refrigerator for about 30 minutes to set the crumb coat.
15. Once the crumb coat is set, divide the remaining frosting into separate bowls and tint each bowl with gel food coloring to create shades of dark blue, purple, pink, and black.
16. Use an offset spatula to spread the colored frosting around the sides and top of the cake in a random, swirling pattern to mimic the appearance of a galaxy.
17. Decorate the cake with edible silver or gold stars, edible silver or gold dust, and edible glitter to enhance the galaxy effect.
18. Slice and serve the galaxy cake, and enjoy the mesmerizing and delicious dessert!

This galaxy cake is sure to be a hit at any special occasion with its celestial-inspired design and rich chocolate flavor. Feel free to customize the colors and decorations to suit your preferences and occasion.

Watercolor Buttercream Cake

Ingredients:

For the cake layers:

- 2 cups all-purpose flour
- 1 3/4 cups granulated sugar
- 1 tablespoon baking powder
- 1/2 teaspoon salt
- 3/4 cup unsalted butter, softened
- 1 cup whole milk
- 4 large eggs, at room temperature
- 1 tablespoon vanilla extract

For the buttercream frosting:

- 3 cups unsalted butter, softened
- 6 cups powdered sugar
- 2 teaspoons vanilla extract
- Pinch of salt
- Gel food coloring in your desired colors for the watercolor effect

Instructions:

1. Preheat your oven to 350°F (175°C). Grease and flour three 8-inch round cake pans and line the bottoms with parchment paper.
2. In a large mixing bowl, sift together the flour, sugar, baking powder, and salt.
3. Add the softened butter to the dry ingredients and mix until the mixture resembles coarse crumbs.
4. In a separate bowl, whisk together the milk, eggs, and vanilla extract.
5. Gradually add the wet ingredients to the dry ingredients, mixing until smooth and well combined.
6. Divide the batter evenly among the prepared cake pans.
7. Bake in the preheated oven for 25-30 minutes, or until a toothpick inserted into the center of the cakes comes out clean.
8. Allow the cakes to cool in the pans for 10 minutes, then transfer them to a wire rack to cool completely.

9. While the cakes are cooling, prepare the buttercream frosting. In a large mixing bowl, beat the butter until creamy. Gradually add the powdered sugar, vanilla extract, and salt. Beat until smooth and creamy.
10. Once the cakes are completely cooled, level the tops if necessary to create flat surfaces.
11. Place one cake layer on a serving plate or cake stand. Spread a layer of frosting on top.
12. Repeat with the remaining layers, stacking them on top of each other.
13. Apply a thin layer of frosting around the entire cake to create a crumb coat. This will seal in any crumbs.
14. Chill the cake in the refrigerator for about 30 minutes to set the crumb coat.
15. Once the crumb coat is set, divide the remaining frosting into separate bowls and tint each bowl with gel food coloring to create your desired watercolor effect.
16. Use an offset spatula to spread the colored frosting around the sides and top of the cake in a random, swirling pattern to mimic the appearance of watercolor.
17. Continue layering and blending the colors until you achieve your desired look.
18. Slice and serve the watercolor buttercream cake, and enjoy the beautiful and delicious dessert!

This cake is sure to impress with its artistic design and rich flavor. Feel free to customize the colors and decorations to suit your preferences and occasion.

Sprinkle Explosion Cake

Ingredients:

For the cake layers:

- 2 cups all-purpose flour
- 1 3/4 cups granulated sugar
- 1 tablespoon baking powder
- 1/2 teaspoon salt
- 3/4 cup unsalted butter, softened
- 1 cup whole milk
- 4 large eggs, at room temperature
- 1 tablespoon vanilla extract

For the frosting:

- 3 cups unsalted butter, softened
- 6 cups powdered sugar
- 2 teaspoons vanilla extract
- Pinch of salt
- Gel food coloring in your desired colors (optional)

For the sprinkle explosion:

- Assorted sprinkles, jimmies, nonpareils, and confetti in various colors and shapes

Instructions:

1. Preheat your oven to 350°F (175°C). Grease and flour three 8-inch round cake pans and line the bottoms with parchment paper.
2. In a large mixing bowl, sift together the flour, sugar, baking powder, and salt.
3. Add the softened butter to the dry ingredients and mix until the mixture resembles coarse crumbs.
4. In a separate bowl, whisk together the milk, eggs, and vanilla extract.

5. Gradually add the wet ingredients to the dry ingredients, mixing until smooth and well combined.
6. Divide the batter evenly among the prepared cake pans.
7. Bake in the preheated oven for 25-30 minutes, or until a toothpick inserted into the center of the cakes comes out clean.
8. Allow the cakes to cool in the pans for 10 minutes, then transfer them to a wire rack to cool completely.
9. While the cakes are cooling, prepare the frosting. In a large mixing bowl, beat the butter until creamy. Gradually add the powdered sugar, vanilla extract, and salt. Beat until smooth and creamy. If desired, add gel food coloring to achieve your desired colors.
10. Once the cakes are completely cooled, level the tops if necessary to create flat surfaces.
11. Place one cake layer on a serving plate or cake stand. Spread a layer of frosting on top.
12. Repeat with the remaining layers, stacking them on top of each other.
13. Apply a thin layer of frosting around the entire cake to create a crumb coat. This will seal in any crumbs.
14. Chill the cake in the refrigerator for about 30 minutes to set the crumb coat.
15. Once the crumb coat is set, apply a final layer of frosting around the cake, smoothing it out with a spatula.
16. To create the sprinkle explosion, gently press handfuls of assorted sprinkles onto the sides and top of the cake, allowing them to spill over and create a fun and colorful explosion effect.
17. Continue adding sprinkles until you achieve your desired look.
18. Slice and serve the sprinkle explosion cake, and enjoy the festive and delicious dessert!

This cake is perfect for birthdays, celebrations, or any occasion where you want to add a burst of color and excitement. Feel free to customize the colors and decorations to suit your preferences and theme.

Gold Leaf Cake

Ingredients:

For the cake layers:

- 2 cups all-purpose flour
- 1 3/4 cups granulated sugar
- 1 tablespoon baking powder
- 1/2 teaspoon salt
- 3/4 cup unsalted butter, softened
- 1 cup whole milk
- 4 large eggs, at room temperature
- 1 tablespoon vanilla extract

For the frosting:

- 3 cups unsalted butter, softened
- 6 cups powdered sugar
- 2 teaspoons vanilla extract
- Pinch of salt

For the gold leaf decoration:

- Edible gold leaf sheets
- Food-safe tweezers or a clean, dry paintbrush

Instructions:

1. Preheat your oven to 350°F (175°C). Grease and flour three 8-inch round cake pans and line the bottoms with parchment paper.
2. In a large mixing bowl, sift together the flour, sugar, baking powder, and salt.
3. Add the softened butter to the dry ingredients and mix until the mixture resembles coarse crumbs.
4. In a separate bowl, whisk together the milk, eggs, and vanilla extract.
5. Gradually add the wet ingredients to the dry ingredients, mixing until smooth and well combined.

6. Divide the batter evenly among the prepared cake pans.
7. Bake in the preheated oven for 25-30 minutes, or until a toothpick inserted into the center of the cakes comes out clean.
8. Allow the cakes to cool in the pans for 10 minutes, then transfer them to a wire rack to cool completely.
9. While the cakes are cooling, prepare the frosting. In a large mixing bowl, beat the butter until creamy. Gradually add the powdered sugar, vanilla extract, and salt. Beat until smooth and creamy.
10. Once the cakes are completely cooled, level the tops if necessary to create flat surfaces.
11. Place one cake layer on a serving plate or cake stand. Spread a layer of frosting on top.
12. Repeat with the remaining layers, stacking them on top of each other.
13. Apply a thin layer of frosting around the entire cake to create a crumb coat. This will seal in any crumbs.
14. Chill the cake in the refrigerator for about 30 minutes to set the crumb coat.
15. Once the crumb coat is set, apply a final layer of frosting around the cake, smoothing it out with a spatula.
16. To decorate with gold leaf, carefully place the edible gold leaf sheets onto the surface of the cake using food-safe tweezers or a clean, dry paintbrush. Gently press the gold leaf onto the frosting, taking care not to tear it.
17. Continue adding gold leaf until you achieve your desired look, covering the entire surface of the cake or creating a decorative pattern.
18. Slice and serve the gold leaf cake, and enjoy the luxurious and elegant dessert!

This cake is perfect for weddings, anniversaries, or any special occasion where you want to add a touch of opulence and sophistication. Feel free to customize the decorations and frosting flavors to suit your preferences.

Succulent Garden Cake

Ingredients:

For the cake layers:

- 2 cups all-purpose flour
- 1 3/4 cups granulated sugar
- 1 tablespoon baking powder
- 1/2 teaspoon salt
- 3/4 cup unsalted butter, softened
- 1 cup whole milk
- 4 large eggs, at room temperature
- 1 tablespoon vanilla extract

For the frosting:

- 3 cups unsalted butter, softened
- 6 cups powdered sugar
- 2 teaspoons vanilla extract
- Pinch of salt
- Green gel food coloring
- Brown gel food coloring

For the succulent decorations:

- Fondant in various shades of green and brown
- Edible food coloring markers
- Small flower cutters
- Leaf cutters
- Rolling pin
- Cornstarch (for dusting)
- Piping bag and small round piping tip
- Edible glue or water

Instructions:

1. Preheat your oven to 350°F (175°C). Grease and flour three 8-inch round cake pans and line the bottoms with parchment paper.
2. In a large mixing bowl, sift together the flour, sugar, baking powder, and salt.

3. Add the softened butter to the dry ingredients and mix until the mixture resembles coarse crumbs.
4. In a separate bowl, whisk together the milk, eggs, and vanilla extract.
5. Gradually add the wet ingredients to the dry ingredients, mixing until smooth and well combined.
6. Divide the batter evenly among the prepared cake pans.
7. Bake in the preheated oven for 25-30 minutes, or until a toothpick inserted into the center of the cakes comes out clean.
8. Allow the cakes to cool in the pans for 10 minutes, then transfer them to a wire rack to cool completely.
9. While the cakes are cooling, prepare the frosting. In a large mixing bowl, beat the butter until creamy. Gradually add the powdered sugar, vanilla extract, and salt. Beat until smooth and creamy.
10. Divide the frosting into two bowls. Tint one bowl of frosting with green gel food coloring for the succulent leaves and the other with brown gel food coloring for the succulent pots.
11. Once the cakes are completely cooled, level the tops if necessary to create flat surfaces.
12. Place one cake layer on a serving plate or cake stand. Spread a layer of green frosting on top for the succulent leaves.
13. Repeat with the remaining layers, stacking them on top of each other.
14. Apply a thin layer of green frosting around the entire cake to create a crumb coat. This will seal in any crumbs.
15. Chill the cake in the refrigerator for about 30 minutes to set the crumb coat.
16. Once the crumb coat is set, apply a final layer of green frosting around the cake, smoothing it out with a spatula.
17. Roll out the brown fondant to a thickness of about 1/4 inch. Use a round cutter to cut out circles for the succulent pots.
18. Roll out the green fondant to a thickness of about 1/8 inch. Use small flower and leaf cutters to cut out various shapes for the succulent leaves.
19. Use edible food coloring markers to add details to the succulent leaves, such as veins and texture.
20. Attach the succulent leaves to the top of the cake using edible glue or water, arranging them in clusters to resemble a succulent garden.
21. Place the fondant pots on the cake, positioning them among the succulent leaves.
22. Use a piping bag fitted with a small round piping tip to pipe small dots of brown frosting around the base of each succulent pot to resemble soil.

23. Slice and serve the succulent garden cake, and enjoy the beautiful and delicious dessert!

This cake is sure to impress with its intricate succulent garden design and delicious flavor. Feel free to get creative with the shapes and colors of the succulent leaves to make your cake truly unique.

Unicorn Cake

Ingredients:

For the cake layers:

- 2 cups all-purpose flour
- 1 3/4 cups granulated sugar
- 1 tablespoon baking powder
- 1/2 teaspoon salt
- 3/4 cup unsalted butter, softened
- 1 cup whole milk
- 4 large eggs, at room temperature
- 1 tablespoon vanilla extract

For the frosting:

- 3 cups unsalted butter, softened
- 6 cups powdered sugar
- 2 teaspoons vanilla extract
- Pinch of salt
- Gel food coloring in pastel colors (pink, purple, blue, etc.)

For the unicorn decorations:

- Fondant in various colors (white, pastel pink, pastel purple, pastel blue, etc.)
- Edible gold or silver luster dust
- Edible gold or silver edible paint
- Edible food coloring markers
- Small flower cutters
- Rolling pin
- Cornstarch (for dusting)
- Piping bag and small round piping tip
- Edible glue or water
- Edible pearl sprinkles or other decorations

Instructions:

1. Preheat your oven to 350°F (175°C). Grease and flour three 8-inch round cake pans and line the bottoms with parchment paper.
2. In a large mixing bowl, sift together the flour, sugar, baking powder, and salt.
3. Add the softened butter to the dry ingredients and mix until the mixture resembles coarse crumbs.
4. In a separate bowl, whisk together the milk, eggs, and vanilla extract.
5. Gradually add the wet ingredients to the dry ingredients, mixing until smooth and well combined.
6. Divide the batter evenly among the prepared cake pans.
7. Bake in the preheated oven for 25-30 minutes, or until a toothpick inserted into the center of the cakes comes out clean.
8. Allow the cakes to cool in the pans for 10 minutes, then transfer them to a wire rack to cool completely.
9. While the cakes are cooling, prepare the frosting. In a large mixing bowl, beat the butter until creamy. Gradually add the powdered sugar, vanilla extract, and salt. Beat until smooth and creamy.
10. Divide the frosting into separate bowls and tint each bowl with gel food coloring to create pastel colors for the unicorn mane and decorations.
11. Once the cakes are completely cooled, level the tops if necessary to create flat surfaces.
12. Place one cake layer on a serving plate or cake stand. Spread a layer of frosting on top.
13. Repeat with the remaining layers, stacking them on top of each other.
14. Apply a thin layer of frosting around the entire cake to create a crumb coat. This will seal in any crumbs.
15. Chill the cake in the refrigerator for about 30 minutes to set the crumb coat.
16. Once the crumb coat is set, apply a final layer of frosting around the cake, smoothing it out with a spatula.
17. To create the unicorn decorations, roll out the various colored fondant to a thickness of about 1/8 inch. Use small flower cutters to cut out flowers for the unicorn's mane.
18. Use edible food coloring markers to add details to the fondant flowers, such as dots and lines.
19. Roll out white fondant and cut out two ear shapes for the unicorn's ears.
20. Roll out pastel-colored fondant and cut out a horn shape for the unicorn's horn.
21. Use edible gold or silver luster dust or edible paint to paint the unicorn's horn.
22. Attach the fondant flowers to the top of the cake using edible glue or water, arranging them in a flowing mane pattern.

23. Attach the fondant ears and horn to the top of the cake using edible glue or water.
24. Pipe small dots of frosting around the base of the horn to resemble a floral crown.
25. Add edible pearl sprinkles or other decorations to the cake as desired.
26. Slice and serve the unicorn cake, and enjoy the magical and whimsical dessert!

This cake is sure to delight with its enchanting design and delicious flavor. Feel free to customize the colors and decorations to suit your preferences and occasion.

Drip Cake with Macarons

Ingredients:

- 2 8-inch round cake layers (your choice of flavor)
- 1 batch of your favorite frosting (buttercream, ganache, etc.)
- 1 cup of chocolate chips or candy melts (for the drip)
- Macarons (for decoration)

Instructions:

1. Prepare and bake your cake layers according to your chosen recipe. Let them cool completely.
2. Level the tops of the cakes if needed and stack them, filling between the layers with frosting.
3. Apply a thin layer of frosting around the outside of the cake to create a crumb coat. Chill the cake in the refrigerator for about 30 minutes to set the crumb coat.
4. Once the crumb coat is set, apply a thicker layer of frosting around the cake, smoothing it out as much as possible.
5. Melt the chocolate chips or candy melts in the microwave or using a double boiler until smooth and pourable.
6. Let the melted chocolate cool slightly, then pour it over the top edge of the cake, allowing it to drip down the sides.
7. Once you've achieved the desired drips, fill in the top of the cake with more melted chocolate and smooth it out with an offset spatula.
8. Decorate the top of the cake with macarons in any pattern you like.
9. Chill the cake in the refrigerator until the chocolate sets, then it's ready to serve!

Macarons:

Ingredients:

- 100g almond flour
- 100g powdered sugar
- 2 large egg whites, at room temperature
- 65g granulated sugar
- Food coloring (optional)
- Your choice of filling (buttercream, ganache, jam, etc.)

Instructions:

1. Line a baking sheet with parchment paper or a silicone baking mat.
2. Sift together the almond flour and powdered sugar in a bowl. Set aside.
3. In a separate bowl, beat the egg whites with an electric mixer until foamy.
4. Gradually add the granulated sugar to the egg whites while continuing to beat, until stiff peaks form.
5. Gently fold the almond flour mixture into the egg whites until just combined. Be careful not to overmix.
6. If using food coloring, add it to the batter and gently fold until evenly colored.
7. Transfer the batter to a piping bag fitted with a round tip.
8. Pipe small circles of batter onto the prepared baking sheet, spacing them about 1 inch apart.
9. Tap the baking sheet on the counter a few times to release any air bubbles.
10. Let the macarons sit at room temperature for about 30 minutes to form a skin.
11. Preheat the oven to 300°F (150°C). Bake the macarons for 15-18 minutes, or until they are set and have developed feet.
12. Let the macarons cool completely on the baking sheet before removing them.
13. Once cooled, pair up the macaron shells and fill them with your desired filling.
14. Sandwich the filled macarons together and chill them in the refrigerator for at least 24 hours before serving.

Enjoy your delicious drip cake adorned with macarons!

Buttercream Flower Wreath Cake

Ingredients:

- 2 or 3 8-inch round cake layers (your choice of flavor)
- 1 batch of buttercream frosting (enough to fill and cover the cake)
- Gel food coloring (various colors)
- Piping bags
- Flower piping tips (such as Wilton 1M or 2D)
- Assorted fresh flowers (for decoration)

Instructions:

1. Prepare the Cake Layers:
    - Bake your cake layers according to your preferred recipe. Let them cool completely before assembling the cake.
2. Prepare the Buttercream Frosting:
    - Make a batch of buttercream frosting using your favorite recipe. Divide the frosting into smaller portions and tint each portion with gel food coloring to create various flower colors.
3. Assemble the Cake:
    - Level the cake layers if needed, and place one layer on a cake board or serving plate.
    - Spread a layer of buttercream frosting on top of the cake layer.
    - Repeat with the remaining cake layers, stacking them on top of each other with frosting between each layer.
4. Crumb Coat:
    - Apply a thin layer of frosting around the outside of the cake to seal in any crumbs. This is called a crumb coat. Chill the cake in the refrigerator for about 30 minutes to set the crumb coat.
5. Decorate with Buttercream Flowers:
    - Fit a piping bag with a flower piping tip and fill it with one of the colored buttercream frostings.
    - Pipe small flowers around the top edge of the cake, creating a wreath pattern. Start from one side and work your way around the cake.
    - Repeat the piping process with the other colored frostings, alternating flower colors as you go. You can use different flower tips to create variety in the flower shapes.
6. Add Fresh Flowers (Optional):
    - To enhance the floral theme, you can also add fresh flowers to the cake. Choose edible flowers that are safe for consumption and place them strategically around the wreath.
7. Final Touches:
    - Once you're happy with the flower wreath design, you can add additional piping details or decorations if desired.
8. Chill and Serve:
    - Chill the cake in the refrigerator until you're ready to serve it. This will help firm up the buttercream and make it easier to slice.

- When ready to serve, slice the cake and enjoy its beautiful appearance and delicious flavor!

This buttercream flower wreath cake is sure to impress your guests with its stunning design and delightful taste. Feel free to customize the colors and flower styles to suit your preferences and the occasion!

Painted Buttercream Cake

Ingredients and Supplies:

- 2 or 3 8-inch round cake layers (your choice of flavor)
- Buttercream frosting (enough to fill and cover the cake)
- Gel food coloring or edible food paint
- Food-safe paint brushes
- Vodka or clear vanilla extract (for thinning the food coloring)
- Piping bags and tips (optional, for additional decorations)

Instructions:

1. Prepare the Cake Layers:
    - Bake your cake layers according to your preferred recipe. Allow them to cool completely before assembling the cake.
2. Prepare the Buttercream Frosting:
    - Make a batch of buttercream frosting using your favorite recipe. Ensure that it's smooth and creamy for easy spreading and painting.
3. Assemble the Cake:
    - Level the cake layers if needed, and place one layer on a cake board or serving plate.
    - Spread a layer of buttercream frosting on top of the cake layer.
    - Repeat with the remaining cake layers, stacking them on top of each other with frosting between each layer.
4. Crumb Coat:
    - Apply a thin layer of frosting around the outside of the cake to seal in any crumbs. Chill the cake in the refrigerator for about 30 minutes to set the crumb coat.
5. Prepare the Paint:
    - If using gel food coloring, you can thin it out with a small amount of vodka or clear vanilla extract to create edible paint. This will make it easier to paint onto the buttercream surface.
6. Painting the Cake:
    - Use your food-safe paint brushes to create your desired design on the cake. You can paint flowers, abstract patterns, landscapes, or any other design you like.
    - Start with lighter colors as a base and gradually add darker colors for shading and depth. You can also mix colors directly on the cake to create custom shades.

- Take your time and work patiently, allowing each layer of paint to dry before adding more details or additional colors.
- If you make a mistake, you can easily scrape off the painted buttercream and start again.

7. Additional Decorations (Optional):
   - If you want to add extra decorations to the cake, you can use piping bags and tips to pipe buttercream accents, borders, or additional designs.
8. Chill and Serve:
   - Once you're satisfied with the painted design, chill the cake in the refrigerator until the buttercream is firm. This will help preserve the painting and make it easier to slice.
   - When ready to serve, slice the cake and enjoy its beautiful and delicious painted design!

With a painted buttercream cake, you can showcase your creativity and artistic skills while also indulging in a delicious dessert. Have fun experimenting with different painting techniques and designs to create a cake that's truly unique and impressive!

Pinata Cake

Ingredients:

- 2 8-inch round cake layers (your choice of flavor)
- 1 batch of frosting (buttercream, ganache, etc.)
- Candy or small treats for filling
- Additional decorations (sprinkles, icing, etc.)

Instructions:

1. Prepare the Cake Layers:
    - Bake your cake layers according to your preferred recipe. Allow them to cool completely before assembling the cake.
2. Prepare the Filling:
    - Choose your favorite candies or small treats to fill the pinata cake. Make sure they are small enough to fit inside the cake and won't weigh it down too much.
3. Assemble the Cake:
    - Level the cake layers if needed, and place one layer on a cake board or serving plate.
    - Spread a layer of frosting on top of the cake layer, leaving a border around the edge to prevent the filling from spilling out.
    - Place the candies or treats in the center of the frosting layer, making sure to distribute them evenly.
4. Add the Top Layer:
    - Place the second cake layer on top of the filling, pressing down gently to secure it in place.
5. Carve the Center:
    - Use a sharp knife to carefully carve out a small section from the center of the top cake layer. This will create a cavity for the filling.
6. Fill the Cake:
    - Fill the carved-out section with more candies or treats, ensuring that it's completely filled.
7. Frost the Cake:
    - Frost the entire cake with the remaining frosting, covering the filled center completely. You can decorate the cake with additional frosting, sprinkles, or icing as desired.
8. Refrigerate:
    - Chill the cake in the refrigerator for at least 30 minutes to allow the frosting to set and the filling to firm up.

9. Slice and Serve:
   - When ready to serve, slice the cake as you normally would. As each slice is cut, the hidden candies or treats inside the cake will spill out, delighting everyone!
10. Enjoy the Surprise:
    - Watch the joy on your guests' faces as they discover the hidden treasures inside the pinata cake. It's a fun and memorable dessert that's perfect for birthdays, parties, or any special occasion!

With its surprise filling and delicious taste, a pinata cake is sure to be a hit at your next celebration! Feel free to get creative with the flavors and decorations to make it your own.

Marbled Fondant Cake

Ingredients and Supplies:

- 2 or 3 8-inch round cake layers (your choice of flavor)
- Fondant (store-bought or homemade)
- Gel food coloring (various colors)
- Rolling pin
- Cornstarch or powdered sugar (for dusting)
- Fondant smoother
- Sharp knife or pizza cutter
- Water or edible glue

Instructions:

1. Prepare the Cake Layers:
   - Bake your cake layers according to your preferred recipe. Let them cool completely before assembling the cake.
2. Prepare the Fondant:
   - Knead the fondant until it's soft and pliable. If it's too stiff, you can microwave it for a few seconds to soften it up.
   - Divide the fondant into smaller portions, one for each color you want to use for marbling.
3. Color the Fondant:
   - Using gel food coloring, tint each portion of fondant with your desired colors. Start with a small amount of color and gradually add more until you achieve the desired shades. Knead the fondant well to distribute the color evenly.
4. Roll Out the Fondant:
   - Dust your work surface with cornstarch or powdered sugar to prevent the fondant from sticking.
   - Roll out each colored fondant portion into thin sheets using a rolling pin. Aim for a similar thickness for each color.
5. Create the Marble Effect:
   - Lay the rolled-out fondant sheets on top of each other, slightly overlapping them.
   - Gently press down on the stacked fondant sheets to adhere them together.
   - Use your hands to twist and fold the fondant layers to create a marbled effect. Be careful not to overmix, as you want distinct swirls of color.
6. Cover the Cake:

- Roll out the marbled fondant into a large enough circle to cover the entire cake.
- Carefully drape the fondant over the cake, smoothing it down with your hands to remove any air bubbles or wrinkles.
- Use a fondant smoother to further smooth out the surface of the fondant and ensure it adheres well to the cake.

7. Trim Excess Fondant:
    - Use a sharp knife or pizza cutter to trim away any excess fondant from around the base of the cake.
8. Final Touches:
    - If there are any imperfections or seams in the fondant, you can gently blend them with your fingers or a small brush dipped in water or edible glue.
9. Decorate (Optional):
    - Once the fondant is in place, you can further decorate the cake with additional fondant decorations, piping, or edible embellishments.
10. Serve and Enjoy:
    - Your marbled fondant cake is now ready to be served and enjoyed! Slice into it to reveal the beautiful swirls of color inside.

With its striking appearance and delicious taste, a marbled fondant cake is sure to impress your guests at any special occasion. Feel free to experiment with different color combinations and techniques to create a unique and stunning dessert!

Gravity-Defying Cake

Ingredients and Supplies:

- Cake layers (your choice of flavor and size, depending on your design)
- Frosting or buttercream
- Cake support structure (e.g., dowels, straws, or cake pillars)
- Cake board or base
- Modeling chocolate, fondant, or gum paste (for decorations)
- Edible glue or royal icing
- Optional: Additional decorations (sprinkles, edible glitter, etc.)

Instructions:

1. Plan Your Design:
    - Decide on the design and theme of your gravity-defying cake. You can choose from various designs such as floating objects, tilted layers, or objects seemingly suspended in mid-air.
2. Bake and Prepare the Cake Layers:
    - Bake your cake layers according to your chosen recipe and allow them to cool completely.
    - Level and stack the cake layers with frosting or buttercream between each layer. If your design requires multiple tiers, use cake support structures (such as dowels or cake pillars) to support the weight of the upper tiers.
3. Construct the Cake:
    - Once the cake layers are stacked and secured, place them on a sturdy cake board or base.
    - If your design involves tilted layers or floating objects, use cake supports to create the desired effect. Ensure that the supports are securely inserted into the cake and can bear the weight of the decorations.
4. Create Decorations:
    - Use modeling chocolate, fondant, or gum paste to sculpt the decorations for your cake. You can shape them into objects such as animals, flowers, or figures, depending on your chosen theme.
    - Allow the decorations to dry and harden before attaching them to the cake.
5. Attach Decorations:
    - Use edible glue or royal icing to attach the decorations to the cake. Be mindful of the placement and balance of the decorations to maintain the gravity-defying effect.

- If necessary, use additional support structures (such as hidden wires or toothpicks) to secure the decorations in place.
6. Add Additional Decorations (Optional):
    - Enhance the visual appeal of your cake by adding additional decorations such as sprinkles, edible glitter, or piped designs.
7. Final Touches:
    - Once all the decorations are in place, step back and admire your gravity-defying creation! Make any final adjustments as needed to ensure stability and balance.
8. Serve and Enjoy:
    - Your gravity-defying cake is now ready to be showcased and enjoyed! Serve it as the centerpiece of your celebration and watch as your guests marvel at your impressive baking skills.

With careful planning and attention to detail, you can create a stunning gravity-defying cake that will leave a lasting impression on everyone who sees it. Have fun experimenting with different designs and techniques to bring your cake to life!

Candy Land Cake

Ingredients and Supplies:

- Cake layers (your choice of flavor)
- Frosting or buttercream
- Assorted candies and chocolates (gumdrops, lollipops, candy canes, licorice, chocolate bars, etc.)
- Fondant or modeling chocolate (optional, for additional decorations)
- Edible glue or royal icing
- Cake board or base
- Optional: Food coloring, sprinkles, edible glitter, etc.

Instructions:

1. Plan Your Design:
    - Decide on the theme and color scheme for your Candy Land cake. You can draw inspiration from the classic board game or create your own unique candy wonderland.
2. Bake and Prepare the Cake Layers:
    - Bake your cake layers according to your chosen recipe and allow them to cool completely.
    - Level and stack the cake layers with frosting or buttercream between each layer.
3. Frost the Cake:
    - Cover the entire cake with a layer of frosting or buttercream. This will serve as the base for attaching the candy decorations.
4. Decorate with Candy:
    - Use assorted candies and chocolates to decorate the cake, creating a colorful and playful Candy Land scene.
    - Arrange the candies in various patterns and designs, such as creating pathways, borders, or clusters of sweets.
    - Use edible glue or royal icing to attach the candies securely to the cake. Be creative and have fun with the placement!
5. Add Additional Decorations:
    - If desired, use fondant or modeling chocolate to create additional decorations such as trees, flowers, or characters from the Candy Land game.
    - You can also use food coloring, sprinkles, or edible glitter to add extra flair and sparkle to your cake.
6. Create a Candy Border (Optional):

- To give your cake a finished look, consider creating a candy border around the base of the cake. Use candies such as candy canes, licorice, or gumdrops to form the border.
7. Final Touches:
    - Step back and admire your Candy Land creation! Make any final adjustments to the decorations to ensure they are securely attached and evenly distributed.
8. Serve and Enjoy:
    - Your Candy Land cake is now ready to be served and enjoyed! Slice into it and delight in the colorful array of candies and sweet treats.

Creating a Candy Land cake is a delightful and whimsical project that's perfect for birthdays, parties, or any special occasion. Let your imagination soar as you transform your cake into a magical land of sweets!

Chalkboard Cake

Ingredients and Supplies:

- Cake layers (your choice of flavor)
- Buttercream frosting (black or dark gray)
- Fondant or gum paste (white)
- Edible food coloring pens (white or pastel colors)
- Rolling pin
- Cornstarch or powdered sugar (for dusting)
- Cake board or base
- Optional: Additional decorations (such as edible flowers, sprinkles, etc.)

Instructions:

1. Bake and Prepare the Cake Layers:
    - Bake your cake layers according to your chosen recipe and allow them to cool completely.
    - Level and stack the cake layers with buttercream frosting between each layer.
2. Frost the Cake:
    - Cover the entire cake with a layer of black or dark gray buttercream frosting. Smooth the frosting as much as possible to create a flat surface resembling a chalkboard.
3. Roll Out the Fondant:
    - Dust your work surface with cornstarch or powdered sugar to prevent the fondant from sticking.
    - Roll out the white fondant or gum paste into a thin, even layer using a rolling pin.
4. Cover the Cake with Fondant:
    - Carefully drape the rolled-out fondant over the frosted cake, smoothing it down gently with your hands to remove any air bubbles or wrinkles.
    - Trim away any excess fondant from around the base of the cake.
5. Create Chalkboard Texture:
    - Use the back of a small spoon or a cake decorating tool to gently indent the fondant, creating a textured surface resembling a chalkboard. Make random marks and lines to mimic the appearance of a used chalkboard.
6. Write Messages or Draw Designs:
    - Use edible food coloring pens in white or pastel colors to write messages, draw designs, or add doodles to the "chalkboard" surface of the cake.

- Get creative and personalize the cake with names, quotes, or illustrations relevant to the occasion.
7. Add Additional Decorations (Optional):
   - Enhance the appearance of the cake by adding additional decorations such as edible flowers, sprinkles, or fondant decorations in coordinating colors.
8. Final Touches:
   - Step back and admire your chalkboard cake creation! Make any final adjustments to the decorations to ensure they are evenly distributed and visually appealing.
9. Serve and Enjoy:
   - Your chalkboard cake is now ready to be served and enjoyed! Slice into it and marvel at the unique and artistic design.

A chalkboard cake is a fun and creative way to make a statement at your next celebration. Whether you're celebrating a birthday, graduation, or any other special occasion, this unique cake is sure to impress!

Topsy-Turvy Cake

Ingredients and Supplies:

- Cake layers (your choice of flavor)
- Buttercream frosting or ganache
- Cake support structure (such as dowels, cake boards, or cake pillars)
- Cake board or base
- Fondant or modeling chocolate
- Optional: Additional decorations (edible flowers, fondant decorations, etc.)

Instructions:

1. Plan Your Design:
    - Decide on the size and shape of your cake layers and the degree of tilt for each layer. Sketch out your design to visualize how the cake will look.
2. Bake and Prepare the Cake Layers:
    - Bake your cake layers according to your chosen recipe and allow them to cool completely.
    - Level the cake layers if needed to ensure they have an even surface.
3. Create Cake Support Structure:
    - Use cake support structures such as dowels, cake boards, or cake pillars to create the topsy-turvy effect. Cut the support pieces at angles to achieve the desired tilt for each layer.
    - Stack the cake layers on top of each other, inserting the support structures as needed to hold the layers in place. Ensure that each layer is securely supported and stable.
4. Frost the Cake:
    - Frost the cake layers with buttercream frosting or ganache, covering any gaps between the layers and smoothing the surface as much as possible.
5. Cover with Fondant or Modeling Chocolate:
    - Roll out fondant or modeling chocolate into thin sheets and drape them over the cake layers, smoothing them down gently to cover the entire cake.
    - Trim away any excess fondant or modeling chocolate from around the base of the cake.
6. Decorate:
    - Get creative with decorating your topsy-turvy cake! You can add stripes, polka dots, swirls, or any other designs using colored fondant or modeling chocolate.

- Use edible flowers, fondant decorations, or other edible embellishments to further enhance the appearance of the cake.
7. Final Touches:
    - Step back and admire your topsy-turvy cake creation! Make any final adjustments to the decorations to ensure they are evenly distributed and visually appealing.
8. Serve and Enjoy:
    - Your topsy-turvy cake is now ready to be served and enjoyed! Slice into it and marvel at the whimsical design and delicious taste.

Making a topsy-turvy cake requires careful planning and attention to detail, but the end result is a stunning and impressive dessert that's sure to be the highlight of any celebration!

Mermaid Tail Cake

Ingredients and Supplies:

- Cake layers (your choice of flavor)
- Buttercream frosting or ganache
- Fondant or modeling chocolate (in various colors)
- Edible food coloring or gel paste (for tinting fondant)
- Rolling pin
- Cornstarch or powdered sugar (for dusting)
- Mermaid tail silicone mold or template
- Edible glitter or luster dust (optional, for decoration)
- Cake board or base
- Optional: Additional decorations (edible pearls, seashell candies, etc.)

Instructions:

1. Bake and Prepare the Cake Layers:
    - Bake your cake layers according to your chosen recipe and allow them to cool completely.
    - Level the cake layers if needed to ensure they have an even surface.
2. Stack and Frost the Cake:
    - Stack the cake layers on top of each other, alternating with layers of buttercream frosting or ganache between each layer.
    - Frost the entire cake with a thin layer of frosting to create a crumb coat, then chill the cake in the refrigerator for about 30 minutes to set the frosting.
    - Apply a final layer of frosting to the chilled cake, smoothing it out as much as possible.
3. Color and Roll Out Fondant:
    - Divide your fondant into the desired colors for the mermaid tail.
    - Use edible food coloring or gel paste to tint each portion of fondant to your desired shades of blue, green, or purple.
    - Roll out each colored fondant into thin sheets using a rolling pin, dusting your work surface with cornstarch or powdered sugar to prevent sticking.
4. Create the Mermaid Tail:
    - Use a mermaid tail silicone mold or template to shape the fondant into a mermaid tail. Press the fondant firmly into the mold or trace around the template with a sharp knife to cut out the shape.
    - Layer the different colors of fondant to create a marbled or ombre effect on the mermaid tail.

- Use your fingers or a small tool to add texture and details to the fondant, such as scales or fins.
5. Attach the Mermaid Tail to the Cake:
    - Carefully lift the fondant mermaid tail and place it on the side of the frosted cake, positioning it at an angle to create the illusion of a swimming mermaid.
    - Gently press the mermaid tail onto the cake to adhere it securely.
6. Add Additional Decorations:
    - Enhance the mermaid tail cake with additional decorations such as edible pearls, seashell candies, or edible glitter or luster dust for extra sparkle and shine.
    - Get creative with underwater-themed decorations to complete the mermaid look!
7. Final Touches:
    - Step back and admire your mermaid tail cake creation! Make any final adjustments to the decorations to ensure they are evenly distributed and visually appealing.
8. Serve and Enjoy:
    - Your mermaid tail cake is now ready to be served and enjoyed! Slice into it and watch as your guests marvel at the enchanting design and delicious taste.

Creating a mermaid tail cake is a wonderful way to bring a touch of magic and fantasy to your celebration. Have fun experimenting with colors, textures, and decorations to make your mermaid cake truly spectacular!

Cookie Monster Cake

Ingredients and Supplies:

- Cake layers (your choice of flavor)
- Buttercream frosting or ganache (blue)
- Cookies (chocolate chip or any variety)
- Candy eyes or fondant (white)
- Optional: Additional decorations (chocolate chips, sprinkles, etc.)

Instructions:

1. Bake and Prepare the Cake Layers:
    - Bake your cake layers according to your chosen recipe and allow them to cool completely.
    - Level the cake layers if needed to ensure they have an even surface.
2. Stack and Frost the Cake:
    - Stack the cake layers on top of each other, alternating with layers of blue buttercream frosting or ganache between each layer.
    - Frost the entire cake with a thick layer of blue frosting, smoothing it out as much as possible to create a furry texture resembling Cookie Monster's fur.
3. Create the Face:
    - Place two large cookies near the top of the cake to serve as Cookie Monster's eyes.
    - Attach candy eyes or fondant circles to the center of each cookie to create the eyes.
    - Optional: Add additional details such as eyebrows or a mouth using black fondant or frosting.
4. Add Cookies:
    - Decorate the top of the cake with an assortment of cookies, scattering them around Cookie Monster's face to resemble the cookies he loves to eat.
    - You can use chocolate chip cookies, sandwich cookies, or any other variety of cookies you like.
5. Decorate with Additional Details:
    - Add additional decorations to the cake to enhance the Cookie Monster theme. You can sprinkle chocolate chips or sprinkles around the base of the cake to represent cookie crumbs.

- Get creative with decorating the cake board or base, using blue frosting to create waves or bubbles to mimic Cookie Monster's underwater habitat.
6. Final Touches:
    - Step back and admire your Cookie Monster cake creation! Make any final adjustments to the decorations to ensure they are evenly distributed and visually appealing.
7. Serve and Enjoy:
    - Your Cookie Monster cake is now ready to be served and enjoyed! Slice into it and watch as your guests delight in the whimsical design and delicious taste.

Creating a Cookie Monster cake is a fun and festive way to celebrate any occasion. Whether you're a fan of Sesame Street or simply love cookies, this adorable cake is sure to be a hit with everyone!

Woodland Creature Cake

Ingredients and Supplies:

- Cake layers (your choice of flavor)
- Buttercream frosting or ganache
- Fondant or modeling chocolate (in various colors)
- Edible food coloring or gel paste
- Rolling pin
- Cornstarch or powdered sugar (for dusting)
- Woodland creature cookie cutters or templates
- Optional: Edible decorations (flowers, leaves, mushrooms, etc.)

Instructions:

1. Bake and Prepare the Cake Layers:
    - Bake your cake layers according to your chosen recipe and allow them to cool completely.
    - Level the cake layers if needed to ensure they have an even surface.
2. Stack and Frost the Cake:
    - Stack the cake layers on top of each other, alternating with layers of buttercream frosting or ganache between each layer.
    - Frost the entire cake with a thin layer of frosting to create a crumb coat, then chill the cake in the refrigerator for about 30 minutes to set the frosting.
    - Apply a final layer of frosting to the chilled cake, smoothing it out as much as possible.
3. Color and Roll Out Fondant:
    - Divide your fondant into the desired colors for the woodland creatures (such as brown for squirrels, gray for rabbits, etc.).
    - Use edible food coloring or gel paste to tint each portion of fondant to your desired shades.
    - Roll out each colored fondant into thin sheets using a rolling pin, dusting your work surface with cornstarch or powdered sugar to prevent sticking.
4. Cut Out Woodland Creatures:
    - Use woodland creature cookie cutters or templates to cut out the shapes of animals such as squirrels, rabbits, deer, foxes, and owls from the rolled-out fondant.
    - You can also use small fondant or modeling chocolate tools to sculpt the creatures by hand if you prefer.
5. Decorate the Cake:

- Arrange the fondant woodland creatures around the sides or top of the cake, creating a woodland scene.
- Use additional fondant or modeling chocolate to create details such as trees, mushrooms, leaves, or flowers to further enhance the woodland theme.
- Get creative with the placement and arrangement of the decorations to bring your woodland creature cake to life!

6. Final Touches:
   - Step back and admire your woodland creature cake creation! Make any final adjustments to the decorations to ensure they are evenly distributed and visually appealing.
7. Serve and Enjoy:
   - Your woodland creature cake is now ready to be served and enjoyed! Slice into it and watch as your guests marvel at the adorable woodland scene and delicious taste.

Creating a woodland creature cake is a delightful way to celebrate any occasion with a touch of nature and whimsy. Have fun experimenting with colors, textures, and decorations to make your woodland cake truly enchanting!

Llama Cake

Ingredients and Supplies:

- Cake layers (your choice of flavor)
- Buttercream frosting or ganache
- Fondant or modeling chocolate (in various colors)
- Edible food coloring or gel paste
- Rolling pin
- Cornstarch or powdered sugar (for dusting)
- Llama-shaped cake pan or llama-shaped cookie cutter
- Optional: Edible decorations (flowers, cacti, etc.)

Instructions:

1. Bake and Prepare the Cake Layers:
    - Bake your cake layers according to your chosen recipe and allow them to cool completely.
    - Level the cake layers if needed to ensure they have an even surface.
2. Stack and Frost the Cake:
    - Stack the cake layers on top of each other, alternating with layers of buttercream frosting or ganache between each layer.
    - Frost the entire cake with a thin layer of frosting to create a crumb coat, then chill the cake in the refrigerator for about 30 minutes to set the frosting.
    - Apply a final layer of frosting to the chilled cake, smoothing it out as much as possible.
3. Color and Roll Out Fondant:
    - Divide your fondant into the desired colors for the llama (such as white for the body, brown for the fur, etc.).
    - Use edible food coloring or gel paste to tint each portion of fondant to your desired shades.
    - Roll out each colored fondant into thin sheets using a rolling pin, dusting your work surface with cornstarch or powdered sugar to prevent sticking.
4. Cut Out Llama Shapes:
    - Use a llama-shaped cake pan or llama-shaped cookie cutter to cut out the shape of the llama from the rolled-out fondant.
    - You can also use small fondant or modeling chocolate tools to sculpt the llama shape by hand if you prefer.
5. Decorate the Cake:

- Place the fondant llama shape on top of the cake, gently pressing it down to adhere it to the frosting.
- Use additional fondant or modeling chocolate to create details such as facial features, ears, legs, and a tail for the llama.
- Get creative with the placement and arrangement of the decorations to bring your llama cake to life!

6. Optional Decorations:
   - Enhance the llama cake with additional edible decorations such as flowers, cacti, or other elements to create a fun and festive scene.
7. Final Touches:
   - Step back and admire your llama cake creation! Make any final adjustments to the decorations to ensure they are evenly distributed and visually appealing.
8. Serve and Enjoy:
   - Your llama cake is now ready to be served and enjoyed! Slice into it and watch as your guests delight in the adorable llama design and delicious taste.

Creating a llama cake is a delightful way to add a touch of whimsy and charm to any celebration. Have fun experimenting with colors, textures, and decorations to make your llama cake truly special!

Vintage Lace Cake

Ingredients and Supplies:

- Cake layers (your choice of flavor)
- Buttercream frosting or ganache
- Fondant or gum paste (white)
- Edible food coloring or gel paste
- Lace mold or lace impression mat
- Rolling pin
- Cornstarch or powdered sugar (for dusting)
- Optional: Edible pearls, flowers, or other decorations

Instructions:

1. Bake and Prepare the Cake Layers:
    - Bake your cake layers according to your chosen recipe and allow them to cool completely.
    - Level the cake layers if needed to ensure they have an even surface.
2. Stack and Frost the Cake:
    - Stack the cake layers on top of each other, alternating with layers of buttercream frosting or ganache between each layer.
    - Frost the entire cake with a thin layer of frosting to create a crumb coat, then chill the cake in the refrigerator for about 30 minutes to set the frosting.
    - Apply a final layer of frosting to the chilled cake, smoothing it out as much as possible.
3. Color and Roll Out Fondant:
    - Roll out white fondant or gum paste into a thin sheet using a rolling pin, dusting your work surface with cornstarch or powdered sugar to prevent sticking.
    - Use edible food coloring or gel paste to tint the fondant to your desired shade for a vintage lace effect, such as ivory or champagne.
4. Create Lace Design:
    - Press the rolled-out fondant into a lace mold or lace impression mat to create a lace pattern on the fondant.
    - Carefully lift the fondant from the mold or mat and drape it over the frosted cake, smoothing it down gently to adhere it to the frosting.
5. Trim Excess Fondant:
    - Trim away any excess fondant from around the base of the cake using a sharp knife or pizza cutter.

6. Add Additional Details (Optional):
    - Enhance the vintage lace cake with additional decorations such as edible pearls, flowers, or other embellishments to complement the lace design.
    - You can also add ribbon around the base of each cake tier for an extra touch of elegance.
7. Final Touches:
    - Step back and admire your vintage lace cake creation! Make any final adjustments to the decorations to ensure they are evenly distributed and visually appealing.
8. Serve and Enjoy:
    - Your vintage lace cake is now ready to be served and enjoyed! Slice into it and savor the delicate beauty and delicious taste.

Creating a vintage lace cake is a wonderful way to add a touch of timeless elegance to your special occasion. With its intricate lace design and exquisite details, this cake is sure to impress your guests and make any celebration unforgettable!

Tropical Tiki Cake

Ingredients and Supplies:

- Cake layers (your choice of flavor)
- Buttercream frosting or ganache
- Fondant or gum paste (in various tropical colors)
- Edible food coloring or gel paste
- Rolling pin
- Cornstarch or powdered sugar (for dusting)
- Tiki mask cookie cutter or template
- Optional: Edible decorations (tropical fruits, palm leaves, flowers, etc.)

Instructions:

1. Bake and Prepare the Cake Layers:
    - Bake your cake layers according to your chosen recipe and allow them to cool completely.
    - Level the cake layers if needed to ensure they have an even surface.
2. Stack and Frost the Cake:
    - Stack the cake layers on top of each other, alternating with layers of buttercream frosting or ganache between each layer.
    - Frost the entire cake with a thin layer of frosting to create a crumb coat, then chill the cake in the refrigerator for about 30 minutes to set the frosting.
    - Apply a final layer of frosting to the chilled cake, smoothing it out as much as possible.
3. Color and Roll Out Fondant:
    - Divide your fondant or gum paste into various tropical colors (such as shades of green, blue, orange, and yellow).
    - Use edible food coloring or gel paste to tint each portion of fondant to your desired shades.
    - Roll out each colored fondant into thin sheets using a rolling pin, dusting your work surface with cornstarch or powdered sugar to prevent sticking.
4. Cut Out Tiki Masks:
    - Use a Tiki mask cookie cutter or template to cut out the shapes of Tiki masks from the rolled-out fondant.
    - You can also use small fondant or modeling chocolate tools to sculpt the Tiki mask shapes by hand if you prefer.
5. Decorate the Cake:

- Arrange the fondant Tiki masks around the sides or top of the cake, creating a festive Tiki party scene.
- Use additional fondant or gum paste to create details such as palm leaves, tropical fruits, flowers, or other elements to enhance the tropical theme.
- Get creative with the placement and arrangement of the decorations to bring your Tiki cake to life!

6. Optional Decorations:
   - Enhance the Tiki cake with additional edible decorations such as tropical fruits (pineapple, mango, kiwi), palm leaves, or edible flowers to create a lush and vibrant tropical landscape.
7. Final Touches:
   - Step back and admire your Tiki cake creation! Make any final adjustments to the decorations to ensure they are evenly distributed and visually appealing.
8. Serve and Enjoy:
   - Your tropical Tiki cake is now ready to be served and enjoyed! Slice into it and transport your guests to a tropical paradise with its vibrant colors and delicious taste.

Creating a tropical Tiki cake is a fantastic way to add a touch of island flair to your celebration. With its colorful decorations and tropical flavors, this cake is sure to be the centerpiece of any party!

Zebra Striped Cake

Ingredients and Supplies:

- Cake batter (your choice of flavor)
- Black food coloring or gel paste
- White cake batter or vanilla cake batter
- Buttercream frosting or ganache
- Optional: Additional decorations (such as fondant, frosting, sprinkles, etc.)

Instructions:

1. Prepare the Cake Batter:
    - Prepare your cake batter according to your chosen recipe. You can use any flavor you like, but it's best to use a light-colored batter, such as vanilla or white, to create a vivid contrast with the zebra stripes.
    - Divide the cake batter into two portions: one portion for the black stripes and one portion for the white stripes.
2. Color the Black Cake Batter:
    - Add black food coloring or gel paste to one portion of the cake batter until you achieve a deep black color. Mix well to ensure the color is evenly distributed throughout the batter.
3. Assemble the Zebra Stripes:
    - Prepare your cake pans by greasing and flouring them or lining them with parchment paper.
    - Begin by pouring a small amount of the white cake batter into the center of each cake pan.
    - Next, pour a smaller amount of the black cake batter directly into the center of the white batter.
    - Continue alternating between the white and black batter, pouring each new layer directly into the center of the previous layer. As you pour, the batter will naturally spread outwards, creating concentric circles of alternating colors.
4. Bake the Cake:
    - Bake the zebra-striped cake layers according to your recipe's instructions. Keep an eye on them while they bake to ensure they don't overcook.
    - Once baked, allow the cake layers to cool completely before assembling and decorating.
5. Assemble and Frost the Cake:

- Once the cake layers are cooled, assemble them by stacking them on top of each other with layers of buttercream frosting or ganache between each layer.
- Apply a thin layer of frosting to the outside of the cake to create a crumb coat. Chill the cake in the refrigerator for about 30 minutes to set the frosting.
- Apply a final layer of frosting to the chilled cake, smoothing it out as much as possible.

6. Optional Decorations:
    - Get creative with decorating your zebra-striped cake! You can use additional frosting, fondant, or edible decorations to enhance the zebra theme. Consider adding zebra stripes or animal print patterns to the sides of the cake for an extra touch of flair.
7. Serve and Enjoy:
    - Your zebra-striped cake is now ready to be served and enjoyed! Slice into it and marvel at the stunning zebra stripes and delicious taste.

Creating a zebra-striped cake is a fun and impressive way to add a pop of excitement to any celebration. With its bold stripes and eye-catching design, this cake is sure to be a hit with everyone!

Balloon Cake

Ingredients and Supplies:

- Cake layers (your choice of flavor)
- Buttercream frosting or ganache
- Fondant or modeling chocolate
- Edible food coloring or gel paste
- Rolling pin
- Balloon-shaped cookie cutter or template
- Optional: Edible decorations (confetti, sprinkles, etc.)

Instructions:

1. Bake and Prepare the Cake Layers:
    - Bake your cake layers according to your chosen recipe and allow them to cool completely.
    - Level the cake layers if needed to ensure they have an even surface.
2. Stack and Frost the Cake:
    - Stack the cake layers on top of each other, alternating with layers of buttercream frosting or ganache between each layer.
    - Frost the entire cake with a thin layer of frosting to create a crumb coat, then chill the cake in the refrigerator for about 30 minutes to set the frosting.
    - Apply a final layer of frosting to the chilled cake, smoothing it out as much as possible.
3. Color and Roll Out Fondant:
    - Divide your fondant or modeling chocolate into various colors to create the balloons (such as red, blue, green, yellow, etc.).
    - Use edible food coloring or gel paste to tint each portion of fondant to your desired colors.
    - Roll out each colored fondant into thin sheets using a rolling pin, dusting your work surface with cornstarch or powdered sugar to prevent sticking.
4. Cut Out Balloon Shapes:
    - Use a balloon-shaped cookie cutter or template to cut out the shapes of balloons from the rolled-out fondant.
    - You can also use small fondant or modeling chocolate tools to sculpt the balloon shapes by hand if you prefer.
5. Decorate the Cake:
    - Arrange the fondant balloons around the sides or top of the cake, creating a festive balloon bouquet.

- Use additional fondant or modeling chocolate to create details such as balloon strings or bows to enhance the balloon theme.
- Optional: Add edible decorations such as confetti or sprinkles around the base of the cake for an extra touch of festivity.

6. Final Touches:
   - Step back and admire your balloon cake creation! Make any final adjustments to the decorations to ensure they are evenly distributed and visually appealing.
7. Serve and Enjoy:
   - Your balloon cake is now ready to be served and enjoyed! Slice into it and watch as your guests delight in the colorful balloons and delicious taste.

Creating a balloon cake is a joyful and festive way to celebrate any occasion. With its bright colors and playful design, this cake is sure to be the centerpiece of your celebration!

Emoji Cake

Ingredients and Supplies:

- Cake layers (your choice of flavor)
- Buttercream frosting or ganache
- Fondant or modeling chocolate
- Edible food coloring or gel paste
- Rolling pin
- Circle cookie cutters or templates
- Optional: Edible decorations (such as sprinkles, fondant decorations, etc.)

Instructions:

1. Bake and Prepare the Cake Layers:
    - Bake your cake layers according to your chosen recipe and allow them to cool completely.
    - Level the cake layers if needed to ensure they have an even surface.
2. Stack and Frost the Cake:
    - Stack the cake layers on top of each other, alternating with layers of buttercream frosting or ganache between each layer.
    - Frost the entire cake with a thin layer of frosting to create a crumb coat, then chill the cake in the refrigerator for about 30 minutes to set the frosting.
    - Apply a final layer of frosting to the chilled cake, smoothing it out as much as possible.
3. Color and Roll Out Fondant:
    - Divide your fondant or modeling chocolate into various colors to create the emoji faces (such as yellow for classic emojis, plus additional colors for different expressions).
    - Use edible food coloring or gel paste to tint each portion of fondant to your desired colors.
    - Roll out each colored fondant into thin sheets using a rolling pin, dusting your work surface with cornstarch or powdered sugar to prevent sticking.
4. Cut Out Circle Shapes:
    - Use circle cookie cutters or templates to cut out the shapes of emoji faces from the rolled-out fondant.
    - You can also use small fondant or modeling chocolate tools to sculpt the emoji faces by hand if you prefer.
5. Decorate the Cake:

- Arrange the fondant emoji faces on top of the cake, creating a fun and expressive design.
- Use additional fondant or modeling chocolate to create details such as eyes, mouths, and facial expressions to bring the emoji faces to life.
- Optional: Add edible decorations such as sprinkles or fondant decorations around the base of the cake for an extra touch of flair.

6. Final Touches:
    - Step back and admire your emoji cake creation! Make any final adjustments to the decorations to ensure they are evenly distributed and visually appealing.
7. Serve and Enjoy:
    - Your emoji cake is now ready to be served and enjoyed! Slice into it and watch as your guests delight in the playful emoji faces and delicious taste.

Creating an emoji cake is a fun and creative way to express yourself and add a pop of personality to your celebration. With its colorful designs and expressive expressions, this cake is sure to be a hit with everyone!

Puzzle Piece Cake

Ingredients and Supplies:

- Cake layers (your choice of flavor)
- Buttercream frosting or ganache
- Fondant or modeling chocolate
- Edible food coloring or gel paste
- Rolling pin
- Puzzle piece-shaped cake pan or puzzle piece-shaped cookie cutter
- Optional: Edible decorations (such as sprinkles, fondant decorations, etc.)

Instructions:

1. Bake and Prepare the Cake Layers:
   - Bake your cake layers according to your chosen recipe and allow them to cool completely.
   - Level the cake layers if needed to ensure they have an even surface.
2. Stack and Frost the Cake:
   - Stack the cake layers on top of each other, alternating with layers of buttercream frosting or ganache between each layer.
   - Frost the entire cake with a thin layer of frosting to create a crumb coat, then chill the cake in the refrigerator for about 30 minutes to set the frosting.
   - Apply a final layer of frosting to the chilled cake, smoothing it out as much as possible.
3. Color and Roll Out Fondant:
   - Divide your fondant or modeling chocolate into various colors to create the puzzle pieces (such as bright colors like red, blue, yellow, green, etc.).
   - Use edible food coloring or gel paste to tint each portion of fondant to your desired colors.
   - Roll out each colored fondant into thin sheets using a rolling pin, dusting your work surface with cornstarch or powdered sugar to prevent sticking.
4. Cut Out Puzzle Piece Shapes:
   - Use a puzzle piece-shaped cake pan or puzzle piece-shaped cookie cutter to cut out the shapes of puzzle pieces from the rolled-out fondant.
   - You can also use small fondant or modeling chocolate tools to sculpt the puzzle piece shapes by hand if you prefer.
5. Decorate the Cake:
   - Arrange the fondant puzzle pieces on top of the cake, interlocking them together to create a cohesive puzzle design.

- Use additional fondant or modeling chocolate to create details such as puzzle piece knobs or patterns to enhance the puzzle theme.
- Optional: Add edible decorations such as sprinkles or fondant decorations around the base of the cake for an extra touch of flair.
6. Final Touches:
   - Step back and admire your puzzle piece cake creation! Make any final adjustments to the decorations to ensure they are evenly distributed and visually appealing.
7. Serve and Enjoy:
   - Your puzzle piece cake is now ready to be served and enjoyed! Slice into it and watch as your guests delight in the creative puzzle design and delicious taste.

Creating a puzzle piece cake is a fun and imaginative way to celebrate teamwork, unity, or any occasion where you want to emphasize the importance of coming together to solve challenges. With its colorful puzzle pieces and playful design, this cake is sure to be a hit with everyone!

Stained Glass Cake

Ingredients and Supplies:

- Cake layers (your choice of flavor)
- Clear gelatin or isomalt
- Edible food coloring or gel paste
- Piping bags or squeeze bottles
- Parchment paper or acetate sheets
- Optional: Edible decorations (such as edible flowers, gold leaf, etc.)

Instructions:

1. Bake and Prepare the Cake Layers:
    - Bake your cake layers according to your chosen recipe and allow them to cool completely.
    - Level the cake layers if needed to ensure they have an even surface.
2. Prepare the Stained Glass Designs:
    - Choose your desired stained glass designs and print or draw them on parchment paper or acetate sheets. You can find templates online or create your own designs.
    - Place the parchment paper or acetate sheets on a flat surface and tape them down to secure them in place.
3. Create the Stained Glass Candy:
    - Melt clear gelatin or isomalt according to the package instructions until it reaches a liquid consistency.
    - Divide the melted gelatin or isomalt into small bowls and tint each portion with edible food coloring or gel paste to your desired colors.
    - Transfer the colored gelatin or isomalt into piping bags or squeeze bottles.
4. Pipe the Stained Glass Designs:
    - Carefully pipe the colored gelatin or isomalt onto the parchment paper or acetate sheets, following the outlines of your stained glass designs.
    - Fill in the designs with the colored gelatin or isomalt, making sure to create smooth and even layers. You can use toothpicks or skewers to help spread the gelatin or isomalt evenly if needed.
5. Allow the Designs to Set:
    - Let the colored gelatin or isomalt cool and harden completely at room temperature. This may take several hours depending on the thickness of the designs.
6. Assemble the Cake:

- Once the stained glass designs have hardened, carefully peel them off the parchment paper or acetate sheets.
- Arrange the stained glass designs on top of the frosted cake layers, pressing them gently into the frosting to adhere them securely.

7. Optional Decorations:
   - Enhance the stained glass cake with additional edible decorations such as edible flowers, gold leaf, or other embellishments to complement the stained glass designs.
8. Final Touches:
   - Step back and admire your stained glass cake creation! Make any final adjustments to the decorations to ensure they are evenly distributed and visually appealing.
9. Serve and Enjoy:
   - Your stained glass cake is now ready to be served and enjoyed! Slice into it and marvel at the intricate designs and vibrant colors.

Creating a stained glass cake is a beautiful and artistic way to showcase your creativity and impress your guests. With its intricate designs and vibrant colors, this cake is sure to be the centerpiece of any celebration!

Dinosaur Fossil Cake

Ingredients and Supplies:

- Cake layers (your choice of flavor)
- Buttercream frosting or ganache
- Crushed cookies or graham crackers (for the "fossil" dirt)
- Dinosaur fossil molds or cookie cutters
- Fondant or modeling chocolate (optional)
- Edible food coloring or gel paste (optional)
- Optional: Edible decorations (such as dinosaur figurines, edible rocks, etc.)

Instructions:

1. Bake and Prepare the Cake Layers:
    - Bake your cake layers according to your chosen recipe and allow them to cool completely.
    - Level the cake layers if needed to ensure they have an even surface.
2. Stack and Frost the Cake:
    - Stack the cake layers on top of each other, alternating with layers of buttercream frosting or ganache between each layer.
    - Frost the entire cake with a thin layer of frosting to create a crumb coat, then chill the cake in the refrigerator for about 30 minutes to set the frosting.
    - Apply a final layer of frosting to the chilled cake, smoothing it out as much as possible.
3. Create the "Fossil" Dirt:
    - Crush cookies or graham crackers into fine crumbs to resemble dirt or sand.
    - Spread the crushed cookies or graham crackers evenly over the top and sides of the frosted cake to create the "fossil" dirt.
4. Make the Dinosaur Fossils:
    - Use dinosaur fossil molds or cookie cutters to create dinosaur fossil shapes from fondant or modeling chocolate.
    - Alternatively, you can sculpt the dinosaur fossil shapes by hand if you prefer.
5. Add Details (Optional):
    - Use edible food coloring or gel paste to paint the dinosaur fossil shapes to give them a more realistic appearance.
    - You can also add additional details such as cracks or texture to the fossils using small fondant or modeling chocolate tools.

6. Arrange the Fossils on the Cake:
   - Once the dinosaur fossil shapes are ready, arrange them on top of the cake, pressing them gently into the "fossil" dirt to secure them in place.
   - Get creative with the placement of the fossils, overlapping them or arranging them in groups to create a dynamic display.
7. Optional Decorations:
   - Enhance the dinosaur fossil cake with additional edible decorations such as dinosaur figurines, edible rocks, or prehistoric plants to complete the prehistoric scene.
8. Final Touches:
   - Step back and admire your dinosaur fossil cake creation! Make any final adjustments to the decorations to ensure they are evenly distributed and visually appealing.
9. Serve and Enjoy:
   - Your dinosaur fossil cake is now ready to be served and enjoyed! Slice into it and watch as your guests marvel at the prehistoric fossils and delicious taste.

Creating a dinosaur fossil cake is a fantastic way to transport your guests back in time to the age of dinosaurs. With its fossilized decorations and delicious flavor, this cake is sure to be a hit with dinosaur enthusiasts of all ages!

Circus Tent Cake

Ingredients and Supplies:

- Cake layers (your choice of flavor)
- Buttercream frosting or ganache
- Red fondant or modeling chocolate
- White fondant or modeling chocolate
- Edible food coloring or gel paste (optional)
- Rolling pin
- Cornstarch or powdered sugar (for dusting)
- Cake board or serving platter
- Optional: Edible decorations (such as fondant animals, circus performers, etc.)

Instructions:

1. Bake and Prepare the Cake Layers:
    - Bake your cake layers according to your chosen recipe and allow them to cool completely.
    - Level the cake layers if needed to ensure they have an even surface.
2. Stack and Frost the Cake:
    - Stack the cake layers on top of each other, alternating with layers of buttercream frosting or ganache between each layer.
    - Frost the entire cake with a thin layer of frosting to create a crumb coat, then chill the cake in the refrigerator for about 30 minutes to set the frosting.
    - Apply a final layer of frosting to the chilled cake, smoothing it out as much as possible.
3. Color and Roll Out Fondant:
    - Divide your red fondant or modeling chocolate into two portions: one larger portion for the tent and one smaller portion for the details.
    - Roll out the larger portion of red fondant into a thin sheet using a rolling pin, dusting your work surface with cornstarch or powdered sugar to prevent sticking.
4. Create the Circus Tent:
    - Drape the rolled-out red fondant over the frosted cake, gently smoothing it down to adhere it to the frosting.
    - Use your hands or fondant tools to shape the fondant into the form of a circus tent, ensuring that the edges are smooth and even.
5. Add Details:

- Roll out the smaller portion of red fondant into thin ropes and use them to create the stripes on the circus tent.
- Roll out white fondant or modeling chocolate and cut out small shapes to create windows, doors, or other details on the circus tent.
- Attach the fondant details to the circus tent using a small amount of water or edible glue.

6. Optional Decorations:
   - Enhance the circus tent cake with additional edible decorations such as fondant animals, circus performers, or other circus-themed elements to complete the scene.
7. Final Touches:
   - Step back and admire your circus tent cake creation! Make any final adjustments to the decorations to ensure they are evenly distributed and visually appealing.
8. Serve and Enjoy:
   - Your circus tent cake is now ready to be served and enjoyed! Slice into it and watch as your guests marvel at the whimsical design and delicious taste.

Creating a circus tent cake is a delightful way to bring the excitement and magic of the circus to your celebration. With its vibrant colors and playful design, this cake is sure to be a hit with circus enthusiasts of all ages!

Pop Art Cake

Ingredients and Supplies:

- Cake layers (your choice of flavor)
- Buttercream frosting or ganache
- Fondant or modeling chocolate (in bright colors)
- Edible food coloring or gel paste
- Rolling pin
- Cornstarch or powdered sugar (for dusting)
- Templates or stencils of pop art designs (such as comic book speech bubbles, polka dots, stripes, etc.)
- Edible markers or food-safe paintbrushes
- Optional: Edible decorations (such as fondant shapes, edible glitter, etc.)

Instructions:

1. Bake and Prepare the Cake Layers:
    - Bake your cake layers according to your chosen recipe and allow them to cool completely.
    - Level the cake layers if needed to ensure they have an even surface.
2. Stack and Frost the Cake:
    - Stack the cake layers on top of each other, alternating with layers of buttercream frosting or ganache between each layer.
    - Frost the entire cake with a thin layer of frosting to create a crumb coat, then chill the cake in the refrigerator for about 30 minutes to set the frosting.
    - Apply a final layer of frosting to the chilled cake, smoothing it out as much as possible.
3. Color and Roll Out Fondant:
    - Divide your fondant or modeling chocolate into bright colors reminiscent of pop art (such as red, yellow, blue, green, etc.).
    - Use edible food coloring or gel paste to tint each portion of fondant to your desired colors.
    - Roll out each colored fondant into thin sheets using a rolling pin, dusting your work surface with cornstarch or powdered sugar to prevent sticking.
4. Create Pop Art Designs:
    - Use templates or stencils of pop art designs (such as comic book speech bubbles, polka dots, stripes, etc.) to create patterns on the rolled-out fondant.

- Cut out the shapes using sharp knives or fondant cutters, ensuring clean edges.
- Alternatively, you can hand-cut or hand-paint pop art designs directly onto the fondant using edible markers or food-safe paintbrushes.

5. Decorate the Cake:
   - Arrange the pop art designs on top of the frosted cake, layering them and overlapping them to create a dynamic and visually appealing composition.
   - Get creative with the placement and arrangement of the pop art designs, mixing and matching colors and patterns for a bold and striking effect.
6. Optional Decorations:
   - Enhance the pop art cake with additional edible decorations such as fondant shapes, edible glitter, or other embellishments to add texture and dimension to the design.
7. Final Touches:
   - Step back and admire your pop art cake creation! Make any final adjustments to the decorations to ensure they are evenly distributed and visually appealing.
8. Serve and Enjoy:
   - Your pop art cake is now ready to be served and enjoyed! Slice into it and watch as your guests marvel at the vibrant colors and bold designs inspired by the pop art movement.

Creating a pop art cake is a fun and expressive way to celebrate any occasion. With its bright colors and bold patterns, this cake is sure to be a conversation starter and a focal point of your celebration!

Pirate Ship Cake

Ingredients and Supplies:

- Cake layers (your choice of flavor)
- Buttercream frosting or ganache
- Fondant or modeling chocolate
- Edible food coloring or gel paste
- Rolling pin
- Cornstarch or powdered sugar (for dusting)
- Pirate ship cake mold or template
- Optional: Edible decorations (such as fondant sails, pirate figurines, edible gold coins, etc.)

Instructions:

1. Bake and Prepare the Cake Layers:
    - Bake your cake layers according to your chosen recipe and allow them to cool completely.
    - Level the cake layers if needed to ensure they have an even surface.
2. Stack and Frost the Cake:
    - Stack the cake layers on top of each other, alternating with layers of buttercream frosting or ganache between each layer.
    - Frost the entire cake with a thin layer of frosting to create a crumb coat, then chill the cake in the refrigerator for about 30 minutes to set the frosting.
    - Apply a final layer of frosting to the chilled cake, smoothing it out as much as possible.
3. Shape the Pirate Ship:
    - If using a pirate ship cake mold, follow the manufacturer's instructions to create the ship's hull and other details.
    - If not using a mold, use a pirate ship template to carve the cake into the shape of a pirate ship, carving away any excess cake to create the desired shape.
4. Cover with Fondant or Modeling Chocolate:
    - Roll out fondant or modeling chocolate into a thin sheet using a rolling pin, dusting your work surface with cornstarch or powdered sugar to prevent sticking.

- Carefully drape the rolled-out fondant or modeling chocolate over the shaped cake, smoothing it down gently to adhere it to the frosting and trim away any excess.
5. Add Details and Decorations:
    - Use additional fondant or modeling chocolate to create details such as the ship's mast, sails, cannons, and other features.
    - Get creative with the details, adding texture and dimension to bring the pirate ship to life.
    - Optional: Add edible decorations such as fondant sails, pirate figurines, edible gold coins, or other embellishments to enhance the pirate theme.
6. Final Touches:
    - Step back and admire your pirate ship cake creation! Make any final adjustments to the decorations to ensure they are evenly distributed and visually appealing.
7. Serve and Enjoy:
    - Your pirate ship cake is now ready to be served and enjoyed! Slice into it and embark on a delicious adventure with your crew of fellow pirates.

Creating a pirate ship cake is a thrilling and imaginative way to celebrate any occasion. With its detailed design and delicious taste, this cake is sure to be the highlight of your pirate-themed party!

Underwater Sea Creature Cake

Ingredients and Supplies:

- Cake layers (your choice of flavor)
- Buttercream frosting or ganache
- Blue fondant or modeling chocolate
- Fondant or modeling chocolate in various colors (for sea creatures)
- Edible food coloring or gel paste
- Rolling pin
- Cornstarch or powdered sugar (for dusting)
- Sea creature-shaped cookie cutters or templates
- Optional: Edible decorations (such as edible pearls, seaweed, coral, etc.)

Instructions:

1. Bake and Prepare the Cake Layers:
    - Bake your cake layers according to your chosen recipe and allow them to cool completely.
    - Level the cake layers if needed to ensure they have an even surface.
2. Stack and Frost the Cake:
    - Stack the cake layers on top of each other, alternating with layers of buttercream frosting or ganache between each layer.
    - Frost the entire cake with a thin layer of frosting to create a crumb coat, then chill the cake in the refrigerator for about 30 minutes to set the frosting.
    - Apply a final layer of frosting to the chilled cake, smoothing it out as much as possible.
3. Color and Roll Out Fondant:
    - Divide your blue fondant or modeling chocolate into two portions: one larger portion for the ocean and one smaller portion for the details.
    - Roll out the larger portion of blue fondant into a thin sheet using a rolling pin, dusting your work surface with cornstarch or powdered sugar to prevent sticking.
    - Carefully drape the rolled-out blue fondant over the frosted cake, gently smoothing it down to adhere it to the frosting and trimming away any excess.
4. Create Sea Creatures:
    - Use sea creature-shaped cookie cutters or templates to cut out shapes from fondant or modeling chocolate in various colors.

- Get creative with the sea creatures, making fish, seahorses, starfish, octopuses, and other creatures that inhabit the ocean depths.

5. Arrange Sea Creatures on the Cake:
    - Once the sea creatures are ready, arrange them on top of the cake, pressing them gently into the blue fondant to secure them in place.
    - Get creative with the placement of the sea creatures, creating a vibrant underwater scene with different shapes, sizes, and colors.
6. Optional Decorations:
    - Enhance the underwater sea creature cake with additional edible decorations such as edible pearls, seaweed, coral, or other elements to complete the underwater scene.
7. Final Touches:
    - Step back and admire your underwater sea creature cake creation! Make any final adjustments to the decorations to ensure they are evenly distributed and visually appealing.
8. Serve and Enjoy:
    - Your underwater sea creature cake is now ready to be served and enjoyed! Slice into it and dive into a delicious adventure beneath the waves with your guests.

Creating an underwater sea creature cake is a fun and imaginative way to celebrate any occasion. With its colorful sea creatures and ocean-themed design, this cake is sure to make a splash at your ocean-themed party!

Comic Book Cake

Ingredients and Supplies:

- Cake layers (your choice of flavor)
- Buttercream frosting or ganache
- Fondant or modeling chocolate
- Edible food coloring or gel paste
- Rolling pin
- Cornstarch or powdered sugar (for dusting)
- Comic book templates or stencils
- Edible markers or food-safe paintbrushes
- Optional: Edible decorations (such as fondant shapes, speech bubbles, etc.)

Instructions:

1. Bake and Prepare the Cake Layers:
    - Bake your cake layers according to your chosen recipe and allow them to cool completely.
    - Level the cake layers if needed to ensure they have an even surface.
2. Stack and Frost the Cake:
    - Stack the cake layers on top of each other, alternating with layers of buttercream frosting or ganache between each layer.
    - Frost the entire cake with a thin layer of frosting to create a crumb coat, then chill the cake in the refrigerator for about 30 minutes to set the frosting.
    - Apply a final layer of frosting to the chilled cake, smoothing it out as much as possible.
3. Color and Roll Out Fondant:
    - Divide your fondant or modeling chocolate into colors reminiscent of comic book art (such as bright primary colors).
    - Use edible food coloring or gel paste to tint each portion of fondant to your desired colors.
    - Roll out each colored fondant into thin sheets using a rolling pin, dusting your work surface with cornstarch or powdered sugar to prevent sticking.
4. Create Comic Book Panels:
    - Use comic book templates or stencils to create panels on the rolled-out fondant, mimicking the layout of a comic book page.
    - Cut out the panels using sharp knives or fondant cutters, ensuring clean edges.

5. Add Comic Book Art:
   - Use edible markers or food-safe paintbrushes to hand-draw comic book-style art onto the fondant panels.
   - Get creative with the designs, incorporating elements such as speech bubbles, action lines, and onomatopoeia to evoke the feel of a comic book.
6. Decorate the Cake:
   - Arrange the fondant panels on top of the frosted cake, layering them and overlapping them to create a dynamic and visually appealing composition.
   - Get creative with the placement and arrangement of the panels, mixing and matching colors and designs for a bold and striking effect.
7. Optional Decorations:
   - Enhance the comic book cake with additional edible decorations such as fondant shapes, speech bubbles, or other comic book-themed elements to complete the scene.
8. Final Touches:
   - Step back and admire your comic book cake creation! Make any final adjustments to the decorations to ensure they are evenly distributed and visually appealing.
9. Serve and Enjoy:
   - Your comic book cake is now ready to be served and enjoyed! Slice into it and watch as your guests marvel at the dynamic and action-packed design inspired by the world of comic books.

Creating a comic book cake is a fun and imaginative way to celebrate any occasion. With its bold colors and expressive designs, this cake is sure to be a hit with comic book fans of all ages!

Edible Flower Petal Cake

Ingredients and Supplies:

- Cake layers (your choice of flavor)
- Buttercream frosting or ganache
- Edible flowers (such as roses, pansies, violets, etc.)
- Edible food coloring or gel paste (optional)
- Piping bags or squeeze bottles
- Small paintbrushes (food-safe)
- Optional: Edible decorations (such as edible pearls, gold leaf, etc.)

Instructions:

1. Bake and Prepare the Cake Layers:
   - Bake your cake layers according to your chosen recipe and allow them to cool completely.
   - Level the cake layers if needed to ensure they have an even surface.
2. Stack and Frost the Cake:
   - Stack the cake layers on top of each other, alternating with layers of buttercream frosting or ganache between each layer.
   - Frost the entire cake with a thin layer of frosting to create a crumb coat, then chill the cake in the refrigerator for about 30 minutes to set the frosting.
   - Apply a final layer of frosting to the chilled cake, smoothing it out as much as possible.
3. Prepare the Edible Flowers:
   - Carefully wash and dry the edible flowers, removing any green parts or stems.
   - If desired, use edible food coloring or gel paste to tint the flowers to your desired colors using a small paintbrush.
4. Arrange the Flowers:
   - Arrange the edible flowers on top of the frosted cake, covering the entire surface with a dense layer of petals.
   - Get creative with the arrangement of the flowers, mixing different colors and varieties to create a visually stunning display.
   - Press the flowers gently into the frosting to adhere them securely to the cake.
5. Optional Decorations:

- Enhance the edible flower petal cake with additional edible decorations such as edible pearls, gold leaf, or other embellishments to add texture and dimension to the design.
6. Final Touches:
    - Step back and admire your edible flower petal cake creation! Make any final adjustments to the decorations to ensure they are evenly distributed and visually appealing.
7. Serve and Enjoy:
    - Your edible flower petal cake is now ready to be served and enjoyed! Slice into it and marvel at the natural beauty of the flowers as you indulge in each delicious bite.

Creating an edible flower petal cake is a delightful way to celebrate any occasion with elegance and grace. With its stunning floral design and delicious taste, this cake is sure to impress your guests and create lasting memories.

Rainbow Swirl Cake

Ingredients and Supplies:

- Cake batter (your choice of flavor)
- Gel food coloring in rainbow colors (red, orange, yellow, green, blue, purple)
- Buttercream frosting or cream cheese frosting
- Piping bags or squeeze bottles
- Optional: Edible decorations (such as rainbow sprinkles, edible glitter, etc.)

Instructions:

1. Prepare the Cake Batter:
    - Prepare your cake batter according to your chosen recipe. Ensure that the batter is evenly divided into separate bowls, one for each color of the rainbow.
2. Color the Batter:
    - Using gel food coloring, tint each bowl of cake batter with a different color of the rainbow. Start with red, then orange, yellow, green, blue, and purple. Mix each color thoroughly until the batter is evenly colored.
3. Prepare the Cake Pans:
    - Grease and flour your cake pans to prevent sticking.
    - Alternatively, you can line the pans with parchment paper for easy removal.
4. Layer the Rainbow Batter:
    - Starting with one color of batter, spoon a small amount into the center of each cake pan.
    - Continue with each color, layering them on top of each other in the center of the pan.
    - As you add each color, gently spread it outwards to create concentric circles of color.
5. Swirl the Colors:
    - Use a butter knife or toothpick to gently swirl the colors together, creating a marbled or swirled effect.
    - Be careful not to overmix, as you want to maintain the distinct colors of the rainbow.
6. Bake the Cake:
    - Bake the cake according to your recipe's instructions, or until a toothpick inserted into the center comes out clean.
    - Allow the cakes to cool completely in the pans before removing them.
7. Frost the Cake:

- Once the cakes are completely cool, level them if necessary to create an even surface.
- Place one layer of cake on a serving plate or cake stand and spread a layer of frosting on top.
- Repeat with the remaining layers of cake and frosting, stacking them on top of each other to create a layered rainbow cake.

8. Decorate (Optional):
    - Decorate the cake with additional edible decorations such as rainbow sprinkles, edible glitter, or fondant decorations to enhance the rainbow theme.
9. Serve and Enjoy:
    - Your rainbow swirl cake is now ready to be served and enjoyed! Slice into it and marvel at the colorful layers as you indulge in each delicious bite.

Creating a rainbow swirl cake is a fun and festive way to add a splash of color to any celebration. With its vibrant layers and delicious taste, this cake is sure to be a hit with everyone!

Rose Gold Cake

Ingredients and Supplies:

- Cake layers (your choice of flavor)
- Buttercream frosting or ganache
- Edible rose gold luster dust
- Clear alcohol (such as vodka or clear extract)
- Small food-safe paintbrushes
- Optional: Edible decorations (such as edible pearls, fondant flowers, etc.)

Instructions:

1. Prepare the Cake Layers:
   - Bake your cake layers according to your chosen recipe and allow them to cool completely.
   - Level the cake layers if needed to ensure they have an even surface.
2. Stack and Frost the Cake:
   - Stack the cake layers on top of each other, alternating with layers of buttercream frosting or ganache between each layer.
   - Frost the entire cake with a thin layer of frosting to create a crumb coat, then chill the cake in the refrigerator for about 30 minutes to set the frosting.
   - Apply a final layer of frosting to the chilled cake, smoothing it out as much as possible.
3. Mix Rose Gold Paint:
   - In a small bowl, mix together edible rose gold luster dust with a small amount of clear alcohol (such as vodka or clear extract). Stir until the luster dust is fully dissolved and the mixture has a paint-like consistency.
4. Paint the Cake:
   - Using food-safe paintbrushes, carefully paint the surface of the cake with the rose gold mixture.
   - You can create a solid rose gold finish or paint decorative patterns or designs onto the cake, depending on your preference.
   - Take your time and work carefully to ensure even coverage and a smooth finish.
5. Optional Decorations:
   - Enhance the rose gold cake with additional edible decorations such as edible pearls, fondant flowers, or other embellishments to add texture and dimension to the design.
6. Final Touches:

- Step back and admire your rose gold cake creation! Make any final adjustments to the decorations to ensure they are evenly distributed and visually appealing.
7. Serve and Enjoy:
    - Your rose gold cake is now ready to be served and enjoyed! Slice into it and savor the luxurious flavor and elegant design.

Creating a rose gold cake is a sophisticated and stylish way to elevate any celebration. With its shimmering finish and decadent taste, this cake is sure to impress your guests and create lasting memories.

Floral Crown Cake

Ingredients and Supplies:

- Cake layers (your choice of flavor)
- Buttercream frosting or fondant
- Edible flowers (such as roses, daisies, lavender, etc.)
- Floral wire or toothpicks (for securing flowers)
- Flower tape (optional)
- Floral scissors or wire cutters
- Piping bag and decorating tips (optional, for additional decorations)
- Optional: Edible glitter, edible pearls, or other edible decorations

Instructions:

1. Bake and Prepare the Cake Layers:
    - Bake your cake layers according to your chosen recipe and allow them to cool completely.
    - Level the cake layers if needed to ensure they have an even surface.
2. Stack and Frost the Cake:
    - Stack the cake layers on top of each other, alternating with layers of buttercream frosting or fondant between each layer.
    - Frost the entire cake with a thin layer of frosting or fondant to create a smooth surface for decorating.
    - Chill the cake in the refrigerator for about 30 minutes to set the frosting or fondant.
3. Prepare the Edible Flowers:
    - Carefully wash and dry the edible flowers, removing any green parts or stems.
    - If using large flowers, such as roses, carefully remove the petals from the stems.
    - If using smaller flowers, leave them attached to the stems for easier placement on the cake.
4. Create the Floral Crown:
    - Arrange the edible flowers around the top edge of the cake to create a floral crown.
    - Start by placing larger flowers evenly around the edge of the cake, then fill in any gaps with smaller flowers or greenery.
    - Secure the flowers to the cake using floral wire or toothpicks, inserting them into the cake at a slight angle so they stay in place.

- Optionally, wrap flower tape around the stems of the flowers to create a more cohesive look.
5. Add Additional Decorations (Optional):
    - Enhance the floral crown cake with additional edible decorations such as edible glitter, edible pearls, or other embellishments to add texture and dimension to the design.
    - Use a piping bag and decorating tips to add additional frosting or fondant decorations to the cake if desired.
6. Final Touches:
    - Step back and admire your floral crown cake creation! Make any final adjustments to the decorations to ensure they are evenly distributed and visually appealing.
7. Serve and Enjoy:
    - Your floral crown cake is now ready to be served and enjoyed! Slice into it and marvel at the natural beauty of the floral crown as you indulge in each delicious bite.

Creating a floral crown cake is a charming and elegant way to celebrate any occasion. With its delicate flowers and decadent taste, this cake is sure to be a hit with your guests and create lasting memories.

Avocado Cake

Ingredients:

- 2 ripe avocados, mashed
- 1 1/2 cups granulated sugar
- 2 large eggs
- 1 teaspoon vanilla extract
- 2 cups all-purpose flour
- 1/2 cup unsweetened cocoa powder
- 1 teaspoon baking soda
- 1/2 teaspoon baking powder
- 1/2 teaspoon salt
- 1 cup buttermilk (or 1 cup milk mixed with 1 tablespoon lemon juice or vinegar, let sit for 5 minutes)
- 1/2 cup vegetable oil

Instructions:

1. Preheat the Oven:
    - Preheat your oven to 350°F (175°C). Grease and flour two 9-inch round cake pans or line them with parchment paper.
2. Prepare the Avocado Mixture:
    - In a mixing bowl, combine the mashed avocados and granulated sugar. Mix until well combined and creamy.
3. Add Eggs and Vanilla:
    - Add the eggs and vanilla extract to the avocado mixture. Beat until smooth and well incorporated.
4. Combine Dry Ingredients:
    - In a separate bowl, sift together the flour, cocoa powder, baking soda, baking powder, and salt.
5. Mix Wet and Dry Ingredients:
    - Gradually add the dry ingredients to the avocado mixture, alternating with the buttermilk. Mix until just combined.
    - Stir in the vegetable oil until the batter is smooth and well mixed.
6. Pour Batter into Cake Pans:
    - Divide the batter evenly between the prepared cake pans.
7. Bake the Cake:
    - Bake in the preheated oven for 25-30 minutes, or until a toothpick inserted into the center comes out clean.

- Remove the cakes from the oven and let them cool in the pans for 10 minutes. Then, transfer them to a wire rack to cool completely.
8. Frost the Cake (Optional):
    - Once the cakes are completely cooled, frost them with your favorite frosting. Cream cheese frosting or chocolate ganache pairs well with avocado cake.
9. Slice and Serve:
    - Slice the avocado cake and serve it as is or with a dollop of whipped cream or a scoop of ice cream on the side.
    - Enjoy your delicious and unique avocado cake!

Avocado cake is moist, rich, and has a subtle avocado flavor that pairs wonderfully with chocolate. It's a delightful dessert that's sure to impress your family and friends at any gathering.

Camping Tent Cake

Ingredients and Supplies:

- Cake layers (your choice of flavor)
- Buttercream frosting or ganache
- Fondant or modeling chocolate
- Edible food coloring or gel paste
- Rolling pin
- Cornstarch or powdered sugar (for dusting)
- Toothpicks or skewers (for support)
- Optional: Edible decorations (such as fondant trees, campfire, edible figurines, etc.)

Instructions:

1. Bake and Prepare the Cake Layers:
    - Bake your cake layers according to your chosen recipe and allow them to cool completely.
    - Level the cake layers if needed to ensure they have an even surface.
2. Stack and Frost the Cake:
    - Stack the cake layers on top of each other, alternating with layers of buttercream frosting or ganache between each layer.
    - Frost the entire cake with a thin layer of frosting to create a crumb coat, then chill the cake in the refrigerator for about 30 minutes to set the frosting.
    - Apply a final layer of frosting to the chilled cake, smoothing it out as much as possible.
3. Color and Roll Out Fondant:
    - Divide your fondant or modeling chocolate into two portions: one larger portion for the tent and one smaller portion for the details.
    - Roll out the larger portion of fondant into a thin sheet using a rolling pin, dusting your work surface with cornstarch or powdered sugar to prevent sticking.
4. Create the Camping Tent:
    - Cut out the shape of a camping tent from the rolled-out fondant, ensuring that it's large enough to cover the top of the cake and drape down the sides to resemble a tent.

- Carefully drape the fondant over the top of the frosted cake, gently smoothing it down to adhere it to the frosting and trimming away any excess.
- Use toothpicks or skewers to support the fondant if needed, inserting them into the cake to hold the tent shape in place.

5. Add Details:
   - Roll out the smaller portion of fondant into thin ropes and use them to create the seams and other details on the camping tent.
   - You can also add additional details such as windows, doors, or ropes using fondant or edible markers.
6. Optional Decorations:
   - Enhance the camping tent cake with additional edible decorations such as fondant trees, a campfire, edible figurines of campers or woodland animals, or other camping-themed elements to complete the scene.
7. Final Touches:
   - Step back and admire your camping tent cake creation! Make any final adjustments to the decorations to ensure they are evenly distributed and visually appealing.
8. Serve and Enjoy:
   - Your camping tent cake is now ready to be served and enjoyed! Slice into it and enjoy a slice of adventure with your fellow campers.

Creating a camping tent cake is a delightful way to celebrate any outdoor-themed occasion. With its charming design and delicious taste, this cake is sure to be a hit with campers of all ages!

Space Rocket Cake

Ingredients and Supplies:

- Cake batter (your preferred flavor)
- Buttercream frosting or fondant
- Cake pans (various sizes for rocket layers)
- Cake board or serving platter
- Rolling pin
- Cake dowels (for support, optional)
- Edible decorations (such as edible glitter, fondant stars, etc.)
- Food coloring (optional, for tinting frosting or fondant)
- Piping bags and tips (optional, for detailing)

Instructions:

1. Bake the Cake Layers:
    - Prepare your cake batter according to your favorite recipe or use store-bought mix.
    - Pour the batter into appropriately sized cake pans to create the layers of your rocket. You may want one large layer for the body of the rocket and smaller layers for the nose cone and fins.
    - Bake the cakes according to the recipe instructions and let them cool completely.
2. Stack and Assemble the Cake Layers:
    - Once cooled, level each cake layer if necessary to create an even surface.
    - Begin assembling the rocket by stacking the layers on top of each other, using frosting or ganache between each layer to adhere them together.
    - If your rocket cake is tall, consider inserting cake dowels into the layers for support.
3. Shape and Frost the Cake:
    - Carve the stacked layers to create the shape of a rocket. The bottom layer should be wider and taper towards the top for the nose cone.
    - Once shaped, crumb coat the cake with a thin layer of frosting to seal in any crumbs. Chill the cake in the refrigerator for about 30 minutes to set the crumb coat.
    - Apply a final layer of frosting or fondant to cover the entire cake, smoothing it out as much as possible.
4. Decorate the Rocket Cake:

- Use fondant or frosting to add details such as windows, doors, and paneling to the rocket.
- Add stripes, stars, or other designs to make the rocket look more realistic.
- If desired, use edible glitter or shimmer dust to give the rocket a cosmic sparkle.
- Create flames or boosters at the bottom of the rocket using orange and yellow frosting or fondant.

5. Add Finishing Touches:
    - Place the rocket cake on a cake board or serving platter.
    - Surround the rocket with edible decorations such as fondant stars or planets to create a space-themed scene.
    - Use piping bags and tips to add any final details or accents to the cake.
6. Serve and Enjoy:
    - Your space rocket cake is now ready to be enjoyed! Slice into it and watch as your guests marvel at your out-of-this-world creation.

Creating a space rocket cake is a thrilling adventure in itself and is sure to be a hit at any space-themed celebration. Have fun and let your imagination soar as you bring this cosmic creation to life!

Dia de los Muertos Cake

Ingredients and Supplies:

- Cake layers (your choice of flavor)
- Buttercream frosting or fondant
- Edible decorations (such as fondant skulls, flowers, etc.)
- Edible food coloring or gel paste
- Rolling pin
- Cornstarch or powdered sugar (for dusting)
- Piping bags and tips (optional, for detailing)
- Optional: Edible glitter, edible pearls, or other edible decorations

Instructions:

1. Bake and Prepare the Cake Layers:
   - Bake your cake layers according to your chosen recipe and allow them to cool completely.
   - Level the cake layers if needed to ensure they have an even surface.
2. Stack and Frost the Cake:
   - Stack the cake layers on top of each other, alternating with layers of buttercream frosting or fondant between each layer.
   - Frost the entire cake with a thin layer of frosting to create a crumb coat, then chill the cake in the refrigerator for about 30 minutes to set the frosting.
   - Apply a final layer of frosting or fondant to the chilled cake, smoothing it out as much as possible.
3. Create Dia de los Muertos Decorations:
   - Roll out fondant into thin sheets using a rolling pin, dusting your work surface with cornstarch or powdered sugar to prevent sticking.
   - Use skull-shaped cookie cutters or templates to cut out fondant skulls.
   - Roll out additional fondant to create flowers, leaves, and other decorative elements typically seen in Dia de los Muertos celebrations.
4. Color and Decorate the Decorations:
   - Use edible food coloring or gel paste to tint the fondant in vibrant colors typically associated with Dia de los Muertos, such as bright oranges, yellows, pinks, blues, and greens.
   - Use piping bags and tips to add details such as eyes, noses, and mouths to the fondant skulls.
   - Decorate the fondant flowers and leaves with edible glitter, edible pearls, or other edible decorations to add sparkle and dimension.

5. Arrange Decorations on the Cake:
   - Once the decorations are ready, arrange them on top of the frosted cake to create a festive Dia de los Muertos scene.
   - Get creative with the placement of the decorations, mixing and matching colors and designs to create a visually stunning display.
6. Optional Decorations:
   - Enhance the Dia de los Muertos cake with additional edible decorations such as fondant marigolds, sugar skulls, or other traditional elements to complete the celebration.
7. Final Touches:
   - Step back and admire your Dia de los Muertos cake creation! Make any final adjustments to the decorations to ensure they are evenly distributed and visually appealing.
8. Serve and Enjoy:
   - Your Dia de los Muertos cake is now ready to be served and enjoyed! Slice into it and celebrate the vibrant culture and traditions of Mexico with your friends and family.

Creating a Dia de los Muertos cake is a beautiful way to honor and celebrate loved ones who have passed away. With its colorful decorations and delicious taste, this cake is sure to be a centerpiece at your Dia de los Muertos celebration.

Harry Potter Sorting Hat Cake

Ingredients and Supplies:

- Cake layers (your choice of flavor)
- Buttercream frosting or fondant
- Edible decorations (such as fondant or modeling chocolate)
- Edible food coloring or gel paste
- Rolling pin
- Cornstarch or powdered sugar (for dusting)
- Piping bags and tips (optional, for detailing)
- Optional: Edible glitter, edible pearls, or other edible decorations

Instructions:

1. Bake and Prepare the Cake Layers:
   - Bake your cake layers according to your chosen recipe and allow them to cool completely.
   - Level the cake layers if needed to ensure they have an even surface.
2. Stack and Frost the Cake:
   - Stack the cake layers on top of each other, alternating with layers of buttercream frosting or fondant between each layer.
   - Frost the entire cake with a thin layer of frosting to create a crumb coat, then chill the cake in the refrigerator for about 30 minutes to set the frosting.
   - Apply a final layer of frosting or fondant to the chilled cake, smoothing it out as much as possible.
3. Create the Sorting Hat:
   - Use fondant or modeling chocolate to sculpt the shape of the Sorting Hat.
   - Start with a large cone shape for the body of the hat and add details such as wrinkles, folds, and the brim of the hat.
   - Use edible food coloring or gel paste to tint the fondant or modeling chocolate in the appropriate colors for the Sorting Hat, such as brown and black.
4. Decorate the Sorting Hat:
   - Once the Sorting Hat is shaped and colored, add additional details such as the stitching, patches, and any other features seen on the Sorting Hat in the Harry Potter series.
   - Use piping bags and tips to add texture and dimension to the hat, such as piping lines or dots to represent stitching or fabric texture.
5. Place the Sorting Hat on the Cake:

- Carefully place the finished Sorting Hat on top of the frosted cake, ensuring that it is securely positioned in the center.
- You can also add additional decorations around the base of the hat, such as fondant books, wands, or other Harry Potter-themed elements.

6. Optional Decorations:
   - Enhance the Sorting Hat cake with additional edible decorations such as edible glitter, edible pearls, or other edible decorations to add sparkle and dimension to the design.
7. Final Touches:
   - Step back and admire your Harry Potter Sorting Hat cake creation! Make any final adjustments to the decorations to ensure they are evenly distributed and visually appealing.
8. Serve and Enjoy:
   - Your Harry Potter Sorting Hat cake is now ready to be served and enjoyed! Slice into it and transport yourself to the magical world of Hogwarts as you indulge in each delicious bite.

Creating a Harry Potter Sorting Hat cake is a delightful way to celebrate the beloved wizarding world of Harry Potter. With its whimsical design and delicious taste, this cake is sure to enchant Harry Potter fans of all ages.

Vintage Travel Suitcase Cake

Ingredients and Supplies:

- Cake layers (your choice of flavor)
- Buttercream frosting or fondant
- Edible decorations (such as fondant or modeling chocolate)
- Edible food coloring or gel paste
- Rolling pin
- Cornstarch or powdered sugar (for dusting)
- Piping bags and tips (optional, for detailing)
- Optional: Edible glitter, edible pearls, or other edible decorations

Instructions:

1. Bake and Prepare the Cake Layers:
   - Bake your cake layers according to your chosen recipe and allow them to cool completely.
   - Level the cake layers if needed to ensure they have an even surface.
2. Stack and Frost the Cake:
   - Stack the cake layers on top of each other, alternating with layers of buttercream frosting or fondant between each layer.
   - Frost the entire cake with a thin layer of frosting to create a crumb coat, then chill the cake in the refrigerator for about 30 minutes to set the frosting.
   - Apply a final layer of frosting or fondant to the chilled cake, smoothing it out as much as possible.
3. Create the Vintage Suitcase Shape:
   - Use a sharp knife to carve the cake into the shape of a vintage travel suitcase. Start by carving away the corners to create rounded edges, and then shape the top to resemble the lid of a suitcase.
   - Use additional cake scraps or fondant to add height to certain areas if needed to achieve the desired shape.
4. Cover the Cake with Fondant:
   - Roll out fondant into a thin sheet using a rolling pin, dusting your work surface with cornstarch or powdered sugar to prevent sticking.
   - Carefully drape the fondant over the shaped cake, smoothing it down to adhere it to the frosting and trimming away any excess.
   - Use a fondant smoother or your hands to smooth out any wrinkles or air bubbles in the fondant.
5. Add Details to the Suitcase:

- Use fondant or modeling chocolate to create details such as straps, buckles, handles, and clasps on the suitcase.
- You can use edible food coloring or gel paste to tint the fondant in vintage-inspired colors such as brown, beige, or cream.

6. Decorate the Suitcase:
   - Add additional details to the suitcase such as stickers, luggage tags, or destination stamps using edible markers or food coloring.
   - Use piping bags and tips to add texture and dimension to the suitcase, such as piping lines or dots to represent stitching or fabric texture.

7. Optional Decorations:
   - Enhance the vintage travel suitcase cake with additional edible decorations such as edible glitter, edible pearls, or other edible decorations to add sparkle and dimension to the design.

8. Final Touches:
   - Step back and admire your vintage travel suitcase cake creation! Make any final adjustments to the decorations to ensure they are evenly distributed and visually appealing.

9. Serve and Enjoy:
   - Your vintage travel suitcase cake is now ready to be served and enjoyed! Slice into it and embark on a delicious journey filled with memories of adventures past and dreams of adventures to come.

Creating a vintage travel suitcase cake is a delightful way to celebrate the spirit of adventure and wanderlust. With its charming design and delicious taste, this cake is sure to be a hit with travelers of all ages.

www.ingramcontent.com/pod-product-compliance
Lightning Source LLC
LaVergne TN
LVHW081556060526
838201LV00054B/1922